When the Devil is Beating His Wife:

A 90-Day Plan to Recover from Domestic Violence

To Regina,

May God bless
your journey with
His abundant care.

Love

Iris
10-25-13

When the Devil is Beating His Wife:
A 90-Day Plan to Recover from Domestic Violence

By

Iris Cooper and Melanie Houston

ALABASTER BOX
MEDIA GROUP

Columbus, Ohio

Scripture taken from the New King James Version®. Copyright © 1982 by Thomas Nelson, Inc. Used by permission. All rights reserved.

Cover Art by Lisa Cliff, Blind Faith Art

Book Layout by Andre Hawkins, Kenosis Design Innovations

Photography by Shellee Fisher Photography

Edited by Amanda E. Forbes

Library of Congress Control Number: 2013945325

ISBN-13: 978-0-9744146-5-2

Alabaster Box Media Group, 1750 E. Broad Street
Columbus, OH 43203
www.alabasterboxmedia.com

PRAISE FOR *When the Devil is Beating His Wife*

"Chilling and liberating! **When the Devil is Beating His Wife** is a call for action and a platform for so many to have the DO's concerning how to move to their God-given blessings of joy, comfort, and peace of mind. I rest assured our God is saying, 'well done.'"

Rev. Ira G. Turpin, Jr., Author
"The Sin in Robbery-33 Ways We Rob God,"
Greater Mt. Nebo AME Church, Bowie, Maryland

"**When the Devil is Beating His Wife** provides the blueprint for reclaiming the joyful living God intends for each of us while stressing the importance of shattering the silence that allows perpetrators to act with impunity."

M. Delois Strum
President, National Coalition of 100 Black Women, Inc.

"This truly is a must read and a book for **all** women. Eyes have not seen, neither ear heard, nor has it entered into the heart of man what this piece of work shall become."

Min. Valerie Handy, Former Task-Force Member
Columbus Coalition Against Family Violence for
Faith-Based Organizations

When the Devil is Beating His Wife is a reminder that although weapons will be formed against us, they will not prosper.

JoAnna Williamson, Ph.D., J.D., MBA

CONTENTS

THANKS and DEDICATION

Iris: I thank God first for perfectly paving the way to complete this book. I thank my children, Mica and Malik, and my grandson, Malachi, for surrounding me with love and support. I also thank all of my sister-friends who help to make my life abundant. And, I thank my brother and sister, Conrad and Carolyn, who stand beside me like pillars, through every storm and rainbow.

Melanie: I thank my husband, Dan, who gave me the time, space, and support to write this book with Iris. Dan, you push, encourage and press me beyond what I think is possible. More than that, you are always my soft and safe place to lay my head and my past. I pray we walk in and become examples of God's covenant. I also thank my mother for showing her strength and love, and all my covenant girlfriends who stand by me as intercessors and wise counsel.

We extend our thanks to those who gave advice and insight on this important subject. We are most grateful to our focus group, a collection of brave women who either work with women who are victims of domestic violence or are actual survivors of domestic violence: April Alexander, MarLita Bartlett, Melony Brunson, Lisa Cliff, Minister Valerie Handy, Shelly Lewis and Barbara Smoot. We also thank M. Delois Strum, President of the National Coalition of 100 Black Women, Inc. for her strong support for women, equality, and justice, as well as Attorney Janet Green Marbley for sound legal advice. Finally, we thank God for our chance encounter at the WalMart on Main Street that led us to a commitment to this project and what we hope is the beginning of new ventures.

This book is dedicated to women everywhere.

"Domestic violence is the willful intimidation, physical assault, battery, sexual assault, and/or other abusive behavior perpetrated by an intimate partner against another. It is an epidemic affecting individuals in every community, regardless of age, economic status, race, religion, nationality or educational background. Violence against women is often accompanied by emotionally abusive and controlling behavior, and thus is part of a systematic pattern of dominance and control. Domestic violence results in physical injury, psychological trauma, and sometimes death. The consequences of domestic violence can cross generations and truly last a lifetime."

Excerpt from the National Coalition Against Domestic Violence.

FOREWORD

By M. Delois Strum

President, National Coalition of 100 Black Women, Inc.

For women who are victims of domestic violence, women who know someone who is a victim of domestic violence, who suspect a daughter, a niece, a friend, a sister or a coworker has fallen victim to domestic violence, or who have witnessed the shattered remains of a survivor of domestic violence, this book IS for you. Unfortunately, this means it is a book with a message for ALL women, because every woman knows at least one woman who falls into one or more of these categories. All too frequently this person may be a victim or survivor of emotional or physical abuse rained down on her by someone she and her family entrusted with her well-being. Domestic violence is much more than a disappointment; it is an outright act of betrayal that requires its own special version of a twelve-step plan to achieve total healing of the mind, body and spirit.

When the Devil is Beating His Wife provides the blueprint for reclaiming the joyful living God intends for each of us while stressing the importance of shattering the silence that allows perpetrators to act with impunity.

These a-ma-zing authors have ensured a book that will transport the reader from victim to victor and from sympathizer to advocate by providing the biblical basis (scripture) for every chapter of the book, while bringing the reader back to HIS plan and HIS promise for each of us. The action items included herein will make you a stronger woman, a responsive friend, a responsibly empowered survivor and/or a committed defender for yourself or another woman. It provides the path forward and ensures that an abused woman can live her life without looking in the rear-view mirror.

"God's peace...is far more wonderful than the human mind can understand. His peace will keep your thoughts and your hearts quiet and at rest" (Philippians 4:7 TLB).

May God grant each of you the peace HE promised; a peace that surpasses all understanding,

Dee Strum
President
National Coalition of 100 Black Women, Inc.

PREFACE

When the Devil is Beating His Wife is written to help women who know they must leave an abusive relationship and leave quickly—women who need a roadmap to physical, emotional, sexual, and mental safety. Whether you are sixteen or sixty, a military wife in a foreign country, or a housewife with no outside income, this book will help confirm that it's time to leave. Additionally, it provides a ninety-day plan to assist in recovering from the abuse and pain.

An **inspired lifestyle** is the perspective from which we write. As authors, our faith in Christ guides our decisions and gives us the strength to persevere. Therefore, the chapters provide step-by-step instructions on how to get through each phase successfully, with scriptural foundations and anecdotal accounts for how an inspired life can be created.

We recognize that some of you have been taught that marriage is an unbreakable covenant regardless of the marital dynamics and conditions under which you live. Time has a way of changing people, their beliefs, behaviors and goals. In a perfect world, we would learn from our mistakes, improve and make better decisions; however, if you are in an abusive marriage or relationship, take authority to make a decision to live the inspired life God has for you, one that is free from violence or abuse of any kind. If you are in immediate danger, please find a safe place for you and your children. From there, you can pray that your abuser seeks and receives qualified professional help.

The guidelines in this book can provide you with a fresh outlook and a new perspective on a life you deserve. In about ninety days, you can begin to put the past behind and cast away a dysfunctional, self-destructive routine and replace it with a productive, fulfilling life.

If you are presently suffering from an abusive relationship (or know someone who is), please continue to read. The knowledge you will gain can minimize the frustration in recuperating from an injurious relationship or prevent you from staying another minute too long. Within a few months, you can begin redesigning your life the way God intended for you.

Working on this book allowed us, the authors, and other women to examine our memories and place them at the foot of the cross. There, Jesus's blood blankets the memories and allows each of us to walk in marriages or relationships where we strive to be witnesses and examples of God's covenant in the earth. It is our prayer that anyone reading this book will have a better understanding of the impact of domestic violence and how to become free of its dreadful grip. In contrast to and to counteract Satan's job description in John 10:10, Christ came so we can have abundant life—abounding in His peace, blessings, grace, mercy, prosperity, health, and fullness of joy. It is ours for the asking. When we ask, He will give; when we seek Him, we will find Him; when we knock on His door, He will open it wide.

NOTE: This book is written to assist women who are in abusive relationships with men. We are not qualified to speak about domestic violence against same sex partners or women who abuse men, but we encourage you to use the steps and resources provided herein to safely leave your abuser, seek professional help and begin to heal.

INTRODUCTION

THE CROOKED MADE STRAIGHT

"I will bring the blind by a way they did not know; I will lead them in paths they have not known. I will make darkness light before them, and crooked places straight. These things I will do for them, and not forsake them" *(Isaiah 42:15-17).*

Everyone's journey from pain and abuse is different. We make different choices about our lives, our careers, our families, and our faith. We are brought up with different philosophies, values and beliefs; however, by no means does God want us to be miserable. His plan for our lives doesn't include pain and anguish from physical, sexual, and/or psychological abuse. He wants us to live and abide in His Word and through our obedience, find the hope, happiness and future He intends for His children.

If you are a victim of domestic violence, we know what's on your mind: question after question after question. Self-doubt creeps in all hours of the day and night.

How did I wind up in a mess like this? Where were the warning signs? Why did I allow the abuse to continue for so long? Did I do something to deserve this? And, what about the children, they need a father.

After the questions, piercing thoughts show up at the front door of your mind. "We were not equally yoked; I knew he had a dark side. The real *me* is smarter than the one I see in the mirror. My family and friends would be horrified to know what I have endured. I can't tell them; I am too embarrassed to let anyone know how weak I have become. What's more, I am too humiliated to let people know I have allowed Satan to run my life. I don't know how to break free without suffering more danger and I don't know if I can make it alone. I'm afraid I might do something

I will live to regret. I am out of control and I hate him. My income isn't enough to pay my bills. Maybe he is right; no one would ever want to put up with me. By his standards, I'm ugly, I'm fat, and I'm stupid. No one will want me now, especially since I have kids. Maybe this is the best I can expect in life so I should just leave well enough alone."

It's totally amazing how Satan can manifest in your mind. After all, once he has your mind, he has access to your body and soul. You become a robot, afraid to move or think about leaving the abuse in case the next decision you make is worse than the one you made before.

STOP IT! Stop it right now! Don't let the enemy confuse you. When you are confused, you are crippled. Be clear that your future **will** be better than your past. Your best days are ahead, not behind. You are God's daughter, beautiful and intelligent. **Regardless of the circumstances that trapped you in the relationship, abuse is not punishment from God.** God is good, He is kind, and He is full of mercy. Free yourself right now. There is more risk by staying than by moving to the next phase of your life. Look to God, not Satan. God will always make you more than a conqueror, a success in your struggles, and a champion in your challenges.

Just like Esther in the Old Testament, God will strategically place you in the right place at the right time to be blessed in ways you can never imagine. All you need to do is to trust Him; trust that He will free you from the abuse just as He frees everyone in His care. Through your relationship with Him and studying His Word, He makes the crooked places straight: crooked lifestyles, crooked relationships, crooked finances, and crooked thoughts that have led to crooked behaviors.

In the following pages, we teach you how to put the pieces back together of a shattered and crooked life in ninety days. During this time, you can see yourself through a new lens of self-esteem, self-determination and self-control. You can begin to create a "new normal" by following this process.

We are not psychologists or family counselors. In fact, we recommend you make regular visits to a counselor as you go through this process. We are simply women who personally experienced domestic violence, or know someone who has, and ultimately overcame this dilemma by allowing God to lead us from misery to victory. **We believe that with God, the unknown future is better than the known past. Peace of mind is better than fear; the possibility of happiness is better than the certainty of pain and sorrow.** We believe if you allow God to wash you in His love, forgiveness, and grace, you can reach a place of personal satisfaction, self-love, and ultimately purpose and destiny.

Please know that this program is for women who are sure they want to move forward. If this is your current state of mind, we pray you read on and resolve to leave your abuser. This process is similar to withdrawal from drug addiction, being drafted into the armed services, or isolation in a foreign land. In all of these circumstances, you are forced to live without the one(s) to whom you were connected. To this end, you should avoid contact with your abuser. In many respects, this is an exercise in the battle for your mind which depends primarily on faith in God and the belief that **He is your source for all that is important**: food, clothing, shelter, safety, love, and companionship. You name it, He's got it.

Again—this program is for women who are absolutely sure they have had enough. It is for those who must protect themselves and their children from further physical, sexual, or mental abuse. It is for those who know that God will never abandon them, and who are willing to endure a three-month emotional fast to have peace in their lives.

By following this program daily, God reveals more of your beauty, gifts, and talents. **Learn to listen to His still, small voice as He orders your steps and affirms your worth.** You may hear it in another person's story or see it when the rainbow appears after a thunderstorm. Your faith and attentiveness to God's voice increases when you are in His perfect will. As a result, you begin to walk in the inheritance He has already prepared for you. God fills the void left in your life with new people, activities, and virtues you never dreamed you would have.

Of course, you must take responsibility for the implementation of the plan and stay focused each day, all day. This may be the hardest test you will endure. Day by day, hour by hour, minute by minute, you will begin to notice that your days are more fulfilling and peaceful. You will begin each day with excitement about the surprises and blessings God has in store for you, and you will become thankful each night when you lay down to reflect on all you have witnessed or accomplished. You will learn to love the woman in the mirror and come to realize you are on the road to emotional recovery.

The process starts with a **safe** and total withdrawal from your abuser. After ninety days, change should be evident to family and friends. Each day, build upon the changes you made the previous day until you are signed, sealed, and delivered into a new lifestyle.

Follow this process faithfully and if you fall off the wagon, regroup, acknowledge your mistake and start over. The ninety days is an approximate timeframe for recovery when you stick to the plan every day. If you are truly ready to be free of pain, let's get started.

1

WHEN THE DEVIL IS BEATING HIS WIFE

"The Lord is my light and my salvation; whom shall I fear? The Lord is the strength of my life; of whom shall I be afraid...Though war may rise against me, in this I will be confident" (Psalm 27: 1, 3).

The sun shone brightly as the storm continued to beat on the walls of the two-story colonial home complemented by the carriage house, beautiful gardens and gazebo. Tears trickled down Joy's face as she stared at the paradoxical site in the sky. How could the sun shine with the dark clouds, lightning, and wind surrounding it? What was God trying to tell her?

And then she remembered her grandmother's words: "When the sun is shining in the middle of the storm, the devil is beating his wife."

And so it was. Joy went to work each day with a smile on her face, but on occasion makeup covered a bruise or a black eye. No one could ever know the secrets in her home. No one could know how little freedom she enjoyed. No one could know she hated herself for allowing this situation. She deserved a life of freedom and happiness, but it seemed the desires of her heart were beyond her grasp. Now, there were holes in her heart where the love she was saving for better days with Jonathan had slipped away.

Joy knew it was inevitable...she and her twelve-year-old son, Donovan, had to leave their beautiful home, but she needed to have a plan before, during, and after. Unfortunately, there wasn't one available—at least not one she was immediately aware of. She was too embarrassed to ask her friends or family for help because they would jump to rescue her, all the while thinking she was crazy and weak (or so she thought). Her family might even make the consequences worse for her if Jonathan sought revenge. She never knew what would set him off. Most of all, Joy feared word would get out that she was a fake and the identity she displayed to the public was a crafty disguise.

It took a few years, but Joy wasn't ready until she had been punched one time too many. After a public confrontation with Jonathan and his mistress after work, Joy took a beating when he returned home in the early hours of the next morning. There was not enough makeup to conceal the swelling under her eye and she looked horrible. Joy knew it was over and she was ready to move on. She prepared her exit with the advice of an attorney, a domestic violence agency, and weeks of careful Internet research that Jonathan couldn't detect or trace. On her way out of the house with Donovan, she turned her face toward heaven. With a sigh, she began her journey out of bondage and a relationship anchored in violence and pain. In her heart, she knew she needed to trust God. Ultimately, He showed her through the wind, thunder, lightning, and rain that the sun could still shine on her tormented life.

2

FOR BETTER OR WORSE

"Husbands love your wives, just as Christ also loved the church...So husbands ought to love their own wives as their own bodies; he who loves his wife loves himself" *(Ephesians 5:25, 28).*

As she strolled slowly through the grocery store, Eva paid close attention to the list she prepared at home. She only purchased those items on the list, and tried not to spend a nickel more. Ellis would be furious if she spent too much. According to *his* calculations, they were on a tight budget and food was always a variable expense. He allotted an allowance for household expenses, leaving little or nothing for Eva's personal indulgence. Even though their ten-year-old twin daughters, Camille and Cara, loved video games, Eva wasn't allowed to purchase them because it was an unnecessary expense, as was an appointment at the salon, or an evening out with her friends. Momentary escapes were by way of borrowed movies and books from the local library.

Eva never experimented with new recipes for fear of ruining the food or preparing something Ellis disliked. The last time she tried a Caribbean dish, he dumped his plate on the kitchen floor for Sam, the dog, to devour it. Hamburgers, meat loaf, spaghetti, tuna casserole, chicken legs—over and over again. It was pretty boring, but it didn't matter. Cooking was part of the job, even if she didn't enjoy it.

Cleaning, cooking, running the twins here and there, working long hours only to turn over her check chronicled the story of her life, for better or for worse.

It just seemed as though Ellis's life was "for better." He always drove the BMW while she drove the old Corolla. He was immaculate about his hair and nails, making frequent trips to the barber and manicurist. Eva was criticized for and denied appointments at the salon and trips to the dry cleaners; yes, the dry cleaners. All expenditures for groceries or household expenses had to be approved before purchase. Ellis took elaborate vacations called business trips without the family. Eva stayed home and went to the park with the twins. He had money; she was broke. He had fun. She had the children. He had female friends who knew he was available. She avoided her female friends because she was too ashamed that they would discover her unimaginable agony and abuse.

Eva had no authority or privacy. Ellis demanded that all mail remain sealed on his desk until he decided to open it. Eva was crushed the day she discovered Ellis opened and trashed a birthday card from an old friend. Even worse, the home computer was his property, and he controlled most of the passwords and email addresses.

Eva was dying a slow, emotional death and she knew it. She couldn't understand why marriage meant she had to sacrifice personal gratification and privacy, while Ellis controlled every aspect of their lives. Where was it written in the Bible that marriage could exist without agreement? Her parents were married for fifty years and she knew her mother never experienced such treatment.

Drifting down the aisles, Eva reminisced on the early days of dating. When they met, Ellis and Eva instantly became the best of friends. The differences in their personalities seemed to provide the balance both needed. No matter the environment or circumstance, Ellis was in control. He always decided on the restaurant, picked out her wardrobe, and even selected her friends. At first, some of his peculiarities were touching and she looked forward to the look in his eyes when she stepped out of the dressing room in a red mini-dress with her size six figure. In hindsight, Eva realized this was nothing more than his demand for control—control of everything in his pretentious, prideful life. Through the years, she watched him grow anal, selfish, and egotistical, focusing less attention on their marriage and the children and more on his appearance. Even with his inward focus, Ellis frequently made decisions about what was better or worse for her.

In all of the marital turmoil, Eva wasn't perfect. Over time, she developed survival skills that included occasional lying and stashing money in a separate bank account. When she told Ellis she was taking the weekend to help Priscilla, a sick friend in Chicago, she was really escaping to a women's retreat to have some time to herself; to collect her thoughts and consider where she was going and how she was going to get there. With all of the noise in her home life, she realized she had distanced herself from God. Eva was ashamed. She couldn't remember the last time she talked or listened to God. She needed Him to hold her, talk to her, encourage her and tell her everything would be fine. Eva felt she needed to apologize to God because she had ignored Him and mistreated Him in spite of all the miraculous and wonderful things He had done for her. Her children were healthy; she had a good job, and most of the time she was in her right mind. Eva cried when she thought about how unworthy she was to receive God's grace. The realization of how God had prepared her to lean on Him, especially as all the marital plates were spinning in the air, hit Eva like a ton of bricks.

When Eva returned home from her weekend getaway, Ellis didn't have too much to say. Later that evening as they drove home from the twins' soccer game, he turned to her and in a measured tone asked, "So, how is Priscilla doing? Is she feeling any better?"

Eva had to pause and think, and immediately her instincts kicked in. Where is this going? Ellis didn't even like Priscilla. To cover her tracks, she called Priscilla before leaving for the retreat and shared her plan. Eva felt safe knowing her girlfriend would cover for her. What Eva didn't know was that Ellis found Priscilla's number online for their joint cell phone account. He became suspicious when Eva needed to leave so suddenly and called Priscilla's home to verify her whereabouts. The women didn't count on Martin, Priscilla's husband, picking up the phone. When Ellis asked to speak to Eva, Martin was confused.

"Priscilla didn't tell me Eva was coming in town. If she's here, I haven't seen her. Is there something wrong?"

"No, no, nothing wrong. You've been very helpful. Maybe I got the dates mixed up," said Ellis, slamming down the phone.

Once Martin shared Ellis's phone call with Priscilla, she was alarmed and quickly called Eva to let her know the cat was out of the bag. The retreat was held in a remote country lodge with limited cell phone reception and Eva never received Priscilla's message. She wasn't prepared for the confrontation that awaited her.

As Ellis sped up the interstate, Eva felt the tension and anger consuming him. She saw the veins bulging in his neck. Conflict and confrontation were imminent, like the horizon before them. With an "I gotcha" tone, he laid into Eva.

"Girls, your mother left us this weekend, did you know that? Who knows who she was *really* spending time with 'cause she wasn't where she said she was going to be. We can't trust a word she says. Tell us, Eva, why'd you lie?"

"To be honest, I attended a women's retreat. I needed time away to think and get myself together," Eva said, looking out of the passenger window, fearing what might happen next.

"Oh, time away. Is that right? Humph. Why don't you get some more time away right now? Get your ass outta the car!"

"Ellis, please. Don't do this now. Yes, I lied, but I needed some time away or I was going to have a meltdown. I have nothing of my own, no freedom, no happiness, and no money. I have nothing and I can't do this one more day."

"Oh. You want freedom? Didn't you hear me, liar? Get out of my car before I throw you out!"

With that, Ellis suddenly pulled over on the highway shoulder, got out and stomped to the passenger side. He yanked the door open, reached across and unfastened the seatbelt, and wrenched Eva out of the car. He threw her purse at her feet. Cara and Camille began crying. They had witnessed Ellis's temper in the past, and sensed that what was about to happen between their parents wasn't going to be pleasant.

"Please don't hurt Mommy. Please Daddy. Daddy!"

If Eva had a weapon and time to react, someone would have been hurt that day. Stunned from being tossed from the car, she managed to stagger to her feet. By the time she got her bearings, Ellis was back in the car. He peeled away, marking each mile with uncontrolled anger. Eva could see the twins in the rear window, crying. And cry they did, the entire way home and well into the night. Livid, yet too embarrassed to call a friend, Eva hiked the mile or so up the road to a shabby convenience store. There she called a cab and waited inside for it to arrive.

Eva knew that groveling was the only way to deal with Ellis, especially if she wanted to comfort Cara and Camille and make sure they weren't harmed in any way. After years of abuse, Eva still didn't have an inkling of an escape plan and there wasn't enough money in her stash to make a bold, daring move. Was this the sign she prayed for over the weekend to end the relationship? The marriage had turned into a war and it was then Eva began thinking like a warrior.

The orange cab pulled into her driveway and Eva released a heavy sigh. Despair, sprinkled with hate consumed her.

Afar off, the neighbor's dog barked to be let back in the house, and the sounds of crickets greeted her as she walked up the porch steps. A mild breeze pushed her up to the door and she could smell the lavender planted close to the house. She didn't have the garage door opener and if Ellis secured the deadbolt from inside, she was locked out. Sticking the key in and praying the door would open, Eva knew that morning was a long way off and it would be another miserable night with Ellis.

Abusive Behavior Checklist

- Ignores your feelings
- Disrespects you
- Ridicules or insults you then tells you it's a joke, or that you have no sense of humor
- Ridicules your beliefs, religion, race, heritage or class
- Withholds approval, appreciation or affection
- Gives you the silent treatment
- Walks away without answering you
- Criticizes you, calls you names, yells at you
- Humiliates you privately or in public
- Rolls his or her eyes when you talk
- Gives you a hard time about socializing with your friends or family
- Makes you socialize (and keep up appearances) even when you don't feel well
- Seems to make sure that what you really want is exactly what you won't get
- Tells you that you are too sensitive

- Hurts you especially when you are down
- Seems energized by fighting, while fighting exhausts you
- Has unpredictable mood swings, alternating from good to bad for no apparent reason
- Presents a wonderful face to the world and is well liked by outsiders
- Twists your words, somehow turning what you said against you
- Attempts to control decisions, money, even the way you style your hair or wear your clothes
- Complains about how badly you treat him
- Threatens to leave, or threatens to throw you out
- Says things that make you feel good, but does things that make you feel bad
- Ever left you stranded
- Ever threatened to hurt you or your family
- Ever hit or pushed you, even "accidentally"
- Seems to stir up trouble just when you seem to be getting closer to each other
- Abuses something you love: a pet, a child, an object
- Compliments you enough to keep you happy, yet criticizes you enough to keep you insecure
- Promises to never do something hurtful again
- Harasses you about imagined affairs
- Manipulates you with lies and contradictions
- Destroys furniture, punches holes in walls, breaks appliances
- Drives like a road-rage junkie
- Acts immature and selfish, yet accuses you of these behaviors
- Questions your every move and motive, somehow questioning your competence

- Interrupts you; hears but doesn't really listen
- Makes you feel like you can't win; whatever you do is never right
- Uses drugs and/or alcohol, which makes the abuse worse
- Incites you to rage, which is "proof" that you are to blame
- Tries to convince you he or she is "right," while you are "wrong"
- Frequently says things that are later denied or accuses you of misunderstanding
- Treats you like a sex object, or as though sex should be provided on demand regardless of how you feel
- Are there changes in your or your children's behavior? Do they appear frightened, exhausted or on edge?
- Do the children seem to be easily upset?
- Are the children experiencing problems in school or other activities?

Domestic violence is the leading cause of injury to women—more than car accidents, muggings, and rapes combined. (Source http://domesticviolencestatistics.org/domestic-violence-statistics/

3

WHEN THE DEVIL IS BEATING YOU

"No weapon formed against you shall prosper, and every tongue which rises against you in judgment you shall condemn. This is the heritage of the servants of the Lord, and their righteousness is from Me," says the Lord (Isaiah 54:17).

Joy returned home late from work after attending a seminar on women and financial security. She had listened intently, writing everything of value on her legal pad. The time quickly slipped away, but she had made arrangements with her friend, Karen, to pick up Donovan. It was important information; every woman needed to know how to save and invest for her future and her children's education.

She grabbed a few items at the pharmacy and ran into Aminah, her childhood friend whom she hadn't seen in two years. They decided to stop for a glass of iced tea and appetizers to catch up. Donovan was fine and Joy knew Jonathan wouldn't head home for quite some time, if he headed home at all. He worked late and frequently spent the night at the office. Joy wanted to bask in the two-hour window she had without worry and demands.

The trendy downtown restaurant, 5 On The Park, hummed with talkative patrons. Joy and Aminah landed a table near the window with a partial view of the patio and the street. A glass of iced tea and a good friend—except for shoe shopping on a Saturday afternoon, what could be better? They watched the rush-hour crowd scurry to their cars and head home to the suburbs. The rat race had ended for another day.

Most of their exchange was about growing up in Canton, and how they vowed to be best friends forever. Joy could still picture them huddled in the back of the church eating candy and writing notes to the cute boys while the preacher boomed the sermon through the microphone. Church was a refuge, then and now, even though she hadn't attended in a while. With a tinge of guilt, Joy missed the spirit and comfort of the sanctuary filled with people from every walk of life, just like she missed Aminah and her penetrating smile and warm laugh. Their impromptu encounter was just the reprieve Joy needed, and she wondered why she had neglected such an important person in her life.

The women laughed and talked for an hour and then started their goodbyes. "Let's get together real soon," they vowed.

As Joy and Aminah headed to their cars, a tall, familiar male profile approached the restaurant with a woman on his arm. As the couple came further into view, Joy gasped and stopped cold, frozen from disbelief. There was Jonathan, who was supposed to be tied up with work. How could this be? Joy's fury was about to consume her but she didn't want her face to reveal the range of emotions circling inside, especially to Aminah. Her heart felt as if it would leap right out of her chest and explode with rage.

Aminah was flabbergasted. "That's not your husband, is it? Joy, is that Jonathan with another woman!? I thought you told me he was working tonight."

Composing herself, Joy sauntered ahead glaring straight into Jonathan's deep set eyes. The couple couldn't escape, which triggered Jonathan's face to grow vicious and defiant.

"What the hell are you doing here? You are supposed to

be at home with Donovan. I didn't tell you to go anywhere but work and home. Crazy bitch! Get home before I slap you right here!" Jonathan hissed.

Aminah grew hot and without thinking jumped in Jonathan's face. "I know you didn't just call my friend a bitch, you low-life snake. What gives you the right to talk to your wife and the mother of your son like she's a dog?"

"Wife! Wife! J, you told me you were getting rid of her and that you were getting a divorce," shouted the woman on Jonathan's arm. It was obvious she was young and ignorant and her territory was not as secure as she thought.

"Don't listen to her, she's crazy. We have reservations, let's go," snapped Jonathan.

"Jaayyyy, tell your girlfriend you lied. You aren't rid of me; you're not divorced. You aren't even in the process of a divorce," said Joy, angrily pointing her finger three inches from his nose.

Jonathan drew his arm back as if to slap Joy, but a small crowd was forming and he was surrounded by three women in the middle of downtown. Instead, he spit right at Joy's feet.

"That's what I think of you and our marriage."

Without another word, he pushed past Joy and Aminah, and hurried into the restaurant, his mistress tripping on her platform shoes behind him.

Left standing on the sidewalk, Joy was horrified and embarrassed. With nothing left to see, the crowd moved on. What right did Jonathan have to be angry and to speak to her like that in the presence of another woman? She hadn't done anything wrong, except spend a few moments with a friend after work. Undoubtedly Jonathan was cheating and got busted. The nerve! Now he wanted to turn the tables to make her think she was the culprit? No way.

"I suggest you see a lawyer with all this mess going on," piped Aminah, never one to back down from a fight. She

31

couldn't believe what she just witnessed. Joy seemed happy only a few minutes ago. What kind of life was she really living, wondered Aminah?

"Joy, it's your life, but baby girl, I want you to be safe. If you need anything, a place to stay, resources, anything, you call me, anytime. And I can find someone to take care of Jonathan's butt. No questions asked."

"I'm okay, I'm okay. Everything will be fine, Aminah. I'll call you tomorrow. I promise I will," said Joy, nervously fishing the car keys from the bottom of her purse. The only thing on her mind at the moment was to beat Jonathan home so she could begin her exit strategy.

For years, Joy strongly suspected Jonathan was unfaithful. In addition to working late hours, he often stayed out all night and returned home wrinkled, with hints of alcohol and perfume circling his tall frame. One night she even discovered a bruise on his neck, which he said happened at the gym. He was especially mean in the mornings after those late nights, finding fault with everything she and Donovan did. This explained why she was always at the OB/GYN getting a prescription. She thanked God it wasn't more than occasional vaginitis. When confronted, Jonathan adeptly turned the tables.

"I know it's not me, so who have you been screwing? Oh, that's right," he would laugh. "No one would want a woman with your skinny legs anyway."

Jonathan never admitted to the adultery and Joy never pushed it. She didn't want to know the cold, hard truth—it was way too painful. Now it was smacking her right in the face.

For her, like so many women raised in church, marriage was a covenant, for better or worse. Her vows were a commitment to love Jonathan no matter what the circumstances. But how could she love him and hate him at the same time? This conflict burned her heart every time she looked in his eyes. Who had changed? Was it Jonathan or was it Joy? Fifteen years ago, Jonathan could do no wrong. Now, the turmoil in their marriage was making Joy physically and mentally sick. She was in the epicenter of a perfect emotional storm.

And there was Donovan. Joy witnessed the aftermath of broken marriages in her family and didn't want the same testimony for him. Not to mention her career...what was a smart Christian woman like her doing in an abusive, adulterous marriage?

Life was more challenging after Joy received a promotion at work and it was clear Jonathan resented her ascent. As a regional administrator with a staff of five subordinates, she was called upon to meet with clients at lunch and dinner, and sometimes out of town. She worried about Donovan when she was away and wondered if he was happy and safe. She knew he was afraid of his dad and didn't like it one bit when he was in charge.

Money was constantly an issue. Although her income was substantially more than his, Jonathan demanded that all funds be deposited into a central account. She put her career on hold for his when they first married, when he wasn't making a dime as a student. Now, at the end of each month, Jonathan's expenses always exceeded their income and lifestyle. Why should he spend more than their household budget allowed? It wasn't fair and she knew it, but to maintain peace in the house, she kept her lips shut, especially after the time she disagreed about the monthly budget and was knocked into the dresser. The lamp fell on her head as she tumbled to the floor. Her anger surged and thoughts of retaliation filled her mind—the kind of retaliation that lands a woman in jail. She wanted to hurt Jonathan in the worst way and knew she should have called the police. Instead, fear dragged her to the bathroom and locked her inside. There, she cried until she could disguise the bruises from Donovan. He didn't need to worry about her, since he was living in harm's way, too. As Joy applied makeup to cover her puffy eyes, she wondered how and when God would free her from the bondage of a marriage on life support.

Joy stumbled to her car, tears rolling down her face as another tide of indignation swelled within. A steady rain began, masking her tears and sad countenance. Not only did the encounter confirm what she already suspected, she knew there would be a physical confrontation when Jonathan crawled in late that night. Once again, it would be her fault. The last time *she* was thirty minutes late he retaliated by standing her up the next evening for dinner with her executive vice president and his wife. When she returned home and inquired why he didn't show up, Jonathan knocked her in the mouth. Joy didn't have any protection against his wrath; he stood at least a foot taller than she did on her tiptoes. Tonight, he would blame her for not being where she was supposed to and claim that the woman on his arm was just his administrative assistant, even though she was obviously dressed for a night on the town.

Year after year, Joy went through each day feeling like a time bomb, unable to unwind. Stress added lines beneath her eyes from insomnia and her hair was thinning at the crown of her head. She had programmed herself to believe that happiness was an illusion, and a successful day was one without assault or confrontation. She didn't need to be happy. Now Joy realized it was time to get serious and start planning her next move—a strategic move out from under Jonathan's thumb before the hatred that was beginning to boil within consumed her and pushed her to the edge.

The end loomed near and Joy wondered if it was time to put 911 on speed dial. She didn't know how or when it would end, but the marriage was on an uncharted course that was leading to places of more and more violence, not reconciliation and peace.

She used to pray that God would show her how to keep her family together in spite of the abuse and violence. The prayer subject was now beginning to change.

"God, please help me get out of this hell! The devil is in my house and I don't know what to do! You said you would never leave me or forsake me. I am your daughter and I need you right now to order my steps. My son needs you. Deliver us from this situation! In the name of Jesus, deliver us!"

Emotional Abuse Checklist

- Do you have to get permission to socialize with your friends?
- Are you accused of cheating when you leave the house to do errands, etc.?
- Are you afraid to talk about certain topics unless he or she is in a good mood?
- Does he have control over the money and monitor your spending?
- Does he tell you no one else would ever want you?
- Does he threaten to harm himself if you leave him?
- Does he go through your purse or open your mail?
- Does he make disparaging remarks about the way you look or dress?
- Does he use things against you that you've confided to him in the past?
- Does he sabotage your efforts to be involved in pleasant social or family events?
- Does he compare you negatively to other women?
- Are you nervous about being on the phone when he is around?
- Is it okay to return home later than scheduled without being fearful?

- Does it feel more like you have a dad than a partner?
- Does he give you the silent treatment when you want to talk or work things out?
- Does he try to turn the children against you?
- Do you feel manipulated by his kindness or gifts?
- Do you feel obligated to be sexual with your partner?
- Are your activities and interests looked upon as unimportant and trivial?
- Does he sabotage your schedule and outside commitments?

Used by permission of Turning Point Domestic Violence and Sexual Assault Services, (205) 758-0808. December 10, 2012.

4

WHEN THE DEVIL IS BEATING YOUR MOTHER

"Therefore, as God's chosen people, holy and dearly loved, clothe yourselves with compassion, kindness, humility, gentleness and patience. Bear with each other and forgive one another if any of you has a grievance against someone. Forgive as the Lord forgave you. And over all these virtues put on love, which binds them all together in perfect unity" (Colossians 3: 12-14).

The images remain. After more than twenty years, Kaitlyn will never forget the abuse her mother sustained at the hands of her stepfather. She would lie in bed, and upon hearing his footsteps hit the porch, worry if an argument was about to begin, filled with slurred curses and raised voices. No one is perfect and so it was with Kaitlyn's parents. Their home was privy to short tempers and vulgar language that Kaitlyn now understands are demonic forces.

The abuse of her mother took place behind closed doors as well as in public. The display of her stepfather's temper, frequently fueled by alcohol, had no boundaries. Outings with friends and family could quickly turn into a nightmare for her mother and embarrassment for all. The entire family was held prisoner to his need for power as well as his penchant for neglect. Highly intelligent and always able to secure decent jobs, he drank and wasted away much of the money he earned, badly needed for a household of six. It was no life for anyone's family. It was hell.

One incident is burned into Kaitlyn's mind. It was a hot summer day in her working-class neighborhood and she must have been around the age of eight or nine. Every house, with the exception of one or two, was filled with children and teenagers. She and her friends played outside from sun up to well after the sun went down, filling their days with softball, hopscotch, and the occasional Kool-Aid stand. Every child had a bike. And a swing set or an inflatable pool was an asset for the entire neighborhood. They didn't have much, but it didn't take much to make them happy.

Whatever her stepdad was doing or planning to do, prompted her mother to quickly gather Kaitlyn and her siblings and run. Fortuitously, at the end of the block, Mrs. Morris saw what was happening and shepherded the family through her front door, but the stay in her sanctuary was brief. Kaitlyn can only guess that her mother was trying to hide herself and her children from whatever abuse that was about to to ensue. She slightly recalls them taking off again and darting around the corner and up one of the major avenues in the neighborhood. Where are we going, why are we running, wondered Kaitlyn? In her innocent mind, she knew they were in danger from her stepdad.

Several neighbors must have witnessed this bizarre scene. Catching up with the family, Kaitlyn's stepdad forced everyone into the car and off they headed to her maternal grandparents' small and comforting home. Her parents argued during the ten-minute drive while Kaitlyn and her siblings sat silently in the back seat, too afraid and too confused to speak. She didn't like it when her stepdad hollered at her mom and called her names.

Upon arrival at their grandmother's home, her stepdad, with what appeared to be a small knife, forced their grandmother into the back bedroom to get money. Within moments, he left with her unwilling mother, leaving the children with their precious and frazzled grandmother.

Although the details are somewhat hazy, Kaitlyn hasn't forgotten how the abuse spread like spilled milk to her grandmother. Next to God, Grandma loved her family unconditionally, especially her grandchildren. She also loved Peace Lutheran Church, where she was an active member since moving from Missouri. There, she spent much of her time as an usher and member of the adult choir. To think someone, anyone, would want to harm or threaten her, remains beyond Kaitlyn's comprehension. That man, who was supposed to be a protector and provider, hurt her sweet, patient grandmother who was the world to Kaitlyn.

Reflecting back, Kaitlyn doesn't remember her grandfather being in the house and she can only imagine the fear and distress that consumed their home like an explosion of hot air that mid-summer day. Her stepdad must have known Grandpa wouldn't be home when he planned his transgression. Kaitlyn knew Grandpa would never have stood for such an assault and had he been present, he would have put the brakes on the madness taking place that afternoon.

Also a devout Lutheran, Kaitlyn's mother finally took the advice of family, friends, and her pastor and put her stepfather out of the house. One day as they were organizing family photos, Kaitlyn's grandmother came across a picture of her mother and stepfather on their wedding day. A dark shadow blocked most of her mother's frame in the picture. Perhaps it was an overcast day or her grandmother's thumb in the wrong place as she snapped the picture.

Grandma shared, "When I saw that shadow hanging over your mother, it was a sign that she was going to have a hard life with him." The prediction was true. In a span of fifteen years, for better or worse was definitely worse.

Kaitlyn is clear—her stepfather never abused her or her siblings. He gets credit for that. Once divorced, however, he made few child support payments for the four children, causing her mother to work multiple jobs for more than a decade. The fragments of the abuse do however, remain. In her thirties, Kaitlyn found herself in a relationship with someone who was abusive. She had the sense to run and never look back. When Kaitlyn dated, she looked for any behaviors that were similar to what she witnessed as a child. A clenched fist, a raised voice, or angry looks were always signs for alarm.

Memories of how she felt and her mother's emotions are like vapors: present, yet in a constant state of disappearance. Some would say Kaitlyn has blocked out much of what she heard and witnessed, and with that analysis, she offers no argument. Recounting and documenting those dreadful images further magnifies the depths of Satan's hate and Kaitlyn isn't sure it will accomplish much. As a victim of abuse, Kaitlyn knows all too well about fists through the walls, her mother hitting the floor, slipping away with siblings, and the terror placed upon family members as they attempted to keep her mother's life from being ripped to pieces.

The path Kaitlyn now grasps to walk is one of forgiveness. Judgment belongs to God. According to Matthew 18:21-35, forgiveness is a seventy times seven formula. It is eternal just as God's mercy endures forever. For many, forgiveness is a process, especially if hate is involved. It can take years and even decades. For Kaitlyn, it took several years of Christ showing her how He had forgiven her of her sins through His death on the cross. As someone who professed Christianity, she was obligated to forgive others regardless of the manner in which they had transgressed against her. Through the years, Kaitlyn continued to give the memories to God, over and over again.

Frequently at night, when the memories would torment her, she could hear His voice saying, "I died for *your* sins." Eventually, Kaitlyn learned that she had no right to judge and no right to be unforgiving. Her freedom came after she gave Him the burdens, the hurt, and the pain. Then she willingly chose to give that freedom to her stepfather through her forgiveness. Eventually, she was able to tell her stepfather that she forgave him for the things she heard and witnessed as a child.

Children should know unconditional love from their parents, stepparents, or guardians. That is the God-ordained role of a parent or caregiver. Unconditional love is a direct reflection of Christ's love. When love is absent, perverted or dysfunctional, it gives children an inaccurate image of God as Father and allows Satan access to their hearts and minds. Until there is healing in the painful places where the abuse occurred, children will not fully comprehend God's infinite love.

For those who have children and are either a victim or a perpetrator, the damage starts at the first blow. The first curled fist. The first backhand. The first curse word. The first time someone is called out of their name. At least two of Kaitlyn's siblings have struggled with drugs and alcohol, which sadly was passed down from both sides of the family, a generational pattern. Family and friends may not physically see the damage, the hurt, the shame, or the mistrust, but Kaityn's story is supported by the statistics and facts about the after-effects of domestic violence. Family members of the perpetrator may ignore, make excuses or try to cover it up, but the abuse will manifest in low self-esteem, the need for control, drug abuse, alcoholism, violence, and other abnormal behaviors.

While Kaitlyn has blocked out many of the emotions she felt at the time she witnessed her mother's abuse, research suggests that many children do not. Professional counselors can supply the counseling you and your children need to lead productive, healthy lives. God's healing Word is powerful for those who use it and rely on it.

On average, between 1993 and 2004, children under age 12 were residents of households experiencing intimate partner violence in 43% of incidents involving female victims and 25% of incidents involving male victims. (Source: Bureau of Justice Statistics, Intimate Partner Violence in the U.S. 1993-2004, 2006)

5

WHEN THE DEVIL IS BEATING YOUR FRIEND

"A man who has friends must himself be friendly, but there is a friend who sticks closer than a brother" *(Proverbs 18:24).*

va was especially quiet in church that Sunday. She seemed deaf to the melodious sounds of the choir, and blind to the beauty of the sun shining through the stained glass windows. She looked tired, as if she hadn't slept very well. Her clothes were wrinkled, which was unusual. Eva was a paralegal at a law firm and usually looked professional even when she went to the market. Something wasn't right with my girl. I questioned what was going on and she replied, "Oh nothing, I'm just tired. You know how it is sometimes."

I recalled how happy Eva was when she finally got married, although I wasn't particularly enthused about Ellis. His behavior was the talk of the town. When I did see him, he didn't have much to say, as if he was annoyed at my presence. Come to think of it, Eva didn't invite me over much anymore, which was also quite odd. Before she was married, we shopped and ate out several times a month. Lately, the only time I usually saw her was at church. She just wasn't the Eva I knew before she married. She was more withdrawn, quiet, and pensive.

As it turned out, I didn't see Eva at church for several months. I tried calling, but her phone went directly to voicemail at home and on her cell. Rumors were circulating among friends that Ellis was running around town and seen with a much younger woman.

Actually, this was his brand before he married Eva. See, Ellis had quite the reputation. Larger than life, he had to be seen and heard wherever he went. Prior to Eva, he was twice married and divorced, and both wives moved to other cities. We were all surprised when he and Eva started dating since she was quiet and avoided the limelight. The center of attention, Ellis didn't share the spotlight with other men. Those close to him knew he was always in control and popular with the ladies, especially the younger ones.

Months later, my cell phone rang around eleven o'clock in the evening. I rarely pick up late night calls because typically it's bad news. This was different; the caller ID showed it was Eva so I grabbed the phone. I hadn't talked to her in months.

"Eva?"

"Nat, we need help. Can you pick us up at the gas station on Smith Road in ten minutes?"

"Okaaay," I drawled, now sitting straight up and wide awake. "What's going on?"

"Ellis just stomped me. He broke my glasses," she huffed, clearly out of breath and her voice cracking. "I can't see that well and ran out of the house with Camille and Cara and nothing but my cell phone and purse. Damn, my nose is bleeding, too. I don't know what to do, Nat. He's drunk, but I think he passed out. I took a chance to get out of there with the twins. If he knew I left with them and finds me I'm afraid he'll kill me. I can't continue to use my cell phone because he might be tracking me. Please help us! You are all we have. Please!"

In an instant my heart broke. Eva had been holding this inside for months, maybe years. Why in the world didn't she tell me? Why didn't I make her tell me? She is my best friend and I ignored the warning signs. Ellis had a history of bad blood with women, and Eva is now one of the team—the team that races out of the house in the middle of the night to avoid getting beaten or killed. What was she thinking by keeping the abuse a secret? Eva has very little family in town, only an elderly aunt and me. If she had just told me that her marriage was in trouble and Ellis was abusive, I would have helped her prepare for the freedom she deserved. She was there for me when my sister had a stroke, and there isn't anything in this world I won't do to help her.

I know that there is no such thing as a one-time slap in the face, I thought as I threw on a sweatshirt and a pair of sweatpants. Please! If it happened once, it'll happen again. Ellis needs to control Eva, and that's why we haven't been shopping or out to dinner. Oohhh, I can't stand a weak, manipulative, insecure man. Clearly, Ellis is threatened by Eva's outside relationships, more importantly her relationship with Christ, her source of power. Yep, that has to be the reason why Eva stopped coming to church.

Now that she has reached out for help and confirmed my suspicions, never again will I let Ellis put his hands on Eva. As her best friend, it's my responsibility to stand up for Eva and help her regain the life she and the children should be living. Eva is precious to me and our friendship is strong enough to hold the weight of this dilemma. As the wind blustered around my truck, I raced to the gas station. Ellis is a bully and needs to be stopped, even if I have to jump in it.

To Help a Victim of Domestic Violence:

- Plan what you want to say, determine a good time and place to talk.

- Ask questions such as "How can I help you?" "What do you want to do about the situation?" Listen without judgment.

- Do not moralize or criticize. Give the victim plenty of time to answer.

- Don't say, "just get out" – it is not safe advice.

- Let the victim know that you believe that verbal, emotional or physical abuse in a relationship is never acceptable, and is not the victim's fault.

- Provide the victim with information about local resources that can help.

- Develop a resource list for shelter, clothing, food, childcare, money, and whatever else a family might need in an emergency.

- Help victims maintain membership within the community and provide children with scholarships so that they can continue to attend school, camps, youth groups, etc.

Based on reports from ten countries, between 55 and 95 percent of women who had been physically abused by their partners had never contacted non-governmental organizations, shelters, or the police for help. (Source: http://domesticviolencestatistics.org/domestic-violence-statistics/)

6

CONFESSION

"Therefore, if any man be in Christ, he is a new creature; all things are passed away, behold, all things have become new" (2 Corinthians 5:17).

Eva sat still and erect on Natalie's couch. They had just arrived at Natalie's after the rescue mission at the gas station. With Cara and Camille starring at her with wide brown eyes, Eva felt numb and couldn't quite think straight. Instantly, Natalie grasped how miserable Eva had been. Without saying a word, she led Eva to her bedroom and took pictures of her face, neck and back for evidence. Nothing needed to be said. Natalie let her silence and the look in her eyes communicate her care and concern. She gently washed Eva's face, cleaning the blood from her nose. After beating Eva, Ellis had staggered upstairs and passed out on the bed, too drunk to care if she was hurt.

It was a cold evening in late April, with all the wind and precipitation of a December day. The chill everyone was feeling, however, had more to do with the recent turn of events than the weather. As Natalie made hot chocolate for the twins, Eva pondered her next move. Out of Natalie's view, Eva feared Natalie would make assumptions and be judgmental about her lifestyle and her choice to stay with Ellis for so long. Their friendship had sustained them through grief, unemployment, and sickness and she prayed it would support this calamity.

Natalie busied herself in the dimly lit kitchen. She was furious and near tears. What in the world has been going on, she wondered? After all, I was there when Camille and Cara were born. I comforted Eva when her mother passed away. Is our friendship not strong enough for Eva to share her life? Why did I let all those months pass without seeing for myself if Eva was okay?

It's a thin line between caring for a friend and getting in her business. Natalie recalled reading that women can be at a seventy-five percent higher risk of being killed *after* they leave their partners, and her mind raced with plans to keep Eva and the twins safe. She also knew the last thing Eva needed at this time was for anyone to judge her. Inwardly she vowed that she would remain committed to helping Eva and the girls at all cost.

What Natalie didn't realize was Eva's burden of abuse had become a lifestyle. Hiding the abuse was part of Eva's identity, part of her daily routine. It was a job—she had to go to it and get through it. Eva pretended she was happy at work and then prepared for conflict and sadness as she drove home.

Camille and Cara sat quietly, confused and anxious. What was happening between their mom and dad, and why were they at Aunt Natalie's house in the middle of the night? What would happen to their dog, Sam? Would they go to the same school? What would they tell their friends? What about their toys? Would they ever see their dad again? Sensing their confusion, Eva looked fondly at them as she fought back the tears.

"Girls, your dad and I can't live together anymore. It's not your fault. We're not happy and it isn't good for the two of you. I know you have been afraid for me and no one should live with that kind of fear. Right now your dad and I need time alone to find out what's wrong with us. Your dad will still be part of your life, but I'll be with you all the time. We have to pray each morning and each night for ourselves and for him. God will hear our prayers and answer each one when the time is right. But right now, we can't go back to the house. I will take care of you, and don't worry, we'll get Sam. I don't have all the answers tonight but God does. We will get through this. Always remember that God wants us to be happy and not to live in fear."

Natalie and Eva sat at breakfast the next morning. They had set out early to retrieve clothes, a spare pair of eyeglasses, and Eva's Corolla. From there, they shuttled the twins to school. Ellis was nowhere to be found and the house looked as if nothing happened the night before. Natalie checked on Sam and packed clothes and books for the twins, while Eva picked through files for important papers and documents she would need. She devised a schedule to return for Sam and more of their belongings in a few days.

How did domestic violence come to exist in Eva's life? Who opened the door and invited the devil to come into her marriage? When did it all start? The questions circled the café booth as the waitress brought their breakfast. Work could wait.

Like haunting landmarks, the signs leading up to Ellis's escalating abuse were all there. Over time, Eva knew eventually she would be forced to leave the marriage, but she chose to stay out of fear of the unknown and a commitment to a stable home life for the twins. Her father viewed Ellis as controlling, egotistical, harsh and insensitive. He also noticed how greedy and selfish Ellis behaved when asked to participate in family functions. He never wanted to host an event, even on Thanksgiving, complaining about the expense. Eva's friends felt the same way. Chauvinistic, authoritarian, and loudmouth were the words they used to describe Ellis, while Eva made excuses for his behavior.

"Well, he's under a lot of stress at work;" "he's had a hard life, you know;" and "he's a great provider."

Eva never set a standard for the respect she deserved. There was never any bar to be raised. Moreover, she often felt that everything was her fault; she had permitted Ellis to mistreat her for years with no objections. In many ways, it was a one-way relationship. Eva was the helpmate while Ellis helped himself.

Natalie recalled her sister Isabella's painful marriage to a pastor who was verbally and physically abusive. Like Eva, Bella kept the abuse from Natalie until it was almost too late. Bella's reputation as the pastor's wife prevented her from seeking comfort, support, and available community resources. It was a self-imposed solitary confinement and in her mind there wasn't anyone with whom Bella felt she could talk to in confidence. When her husband broke her wrist in a fit of rage, Bella left the marriage, the parsonage, and almost left God. She struggled with depression and didn't step foot in a church for nearly three years. With the help of several years of counseling and therapy, she was finally in a place of healing and restoration. Eventually, she reconciled that even pastors can be abusive. Bella took the bold initiative to start a small care group in her home, comprised of women who were victims of domestic violence. She knew she was blessed to be alive. It was her way of serving as a vessel for women who needed a safe place to land, a place to talk and to be transparent.

Holding hands while Eva shared the secret horrors of her marriage brought tears to the women.

"I'm your friend Eva. That's never, ever gonna change. You can stay with me until you decide what you're going to do. You can depend on me," said Natalie. "Seriously, though, what *are* you going to do? You *need* to call the police and press charges for assault. We have pictures that prove the abuse. Enough is enough. I'll even go with you."

Beating back the tears that continued to flow from a deep well, Eva exhaled. "I know you're right. I can't pretend that I'm happy anymore. I've run out of disguises and excuses. I'm thirty-eight and I've got to take back my life for my sake and the sake of the twins. I don't want them exposed to any more abuse and I don't want them to lose respect for me or think this lifestyle is normal. As it is, I'll need to get them into counseling right away."

"Eva, whether you realize it or not, you're a strong, attractive woman," Natalie said. "You don't deserve this. It's better to be alone in peace than to be tortured in a relationship. No one can endure what you've been through, maintain a house, and raise beautiful girls without faith in God. Don't you remember how God's Word promises us a hope and a future in Jeremiah 29:11? I know that even if I never find Mr. Right, God will take care of me and my needs. That promise is for you, too. Since when did you stop believing God's Word? With Him your possibilities are unlimited. And how long did you really think you could keep this from me?" Natalie hugged her with sisterly love.

"I know I should have shared this with you, but I have been living in fear for the past several years," admitted Eva. "The fear of someone finding out that my marriage is bad. Fear of not being able to support me and the twins. Fear that if we left, Ellis would hunt us down. Fear got up with me every morning and hitched a ride to work. It was always on time whether I was or not. Fear caught a ride back home and hung out with me throughout the weekends. Fear, fear, fear. Nat, you can't tell me he hasn't put software on my phone and our home computer to track my whereabouts. I'm paranoid!"

Eva paused and stared into her coffee cup. "Some fear is necessary and productive, you know," she said looking up. "Fear led me to do research at work and did you know that all you have to do is type "spy on my girlfriend" or "spy on my wife" in any search engine and you'll come up with all kinds of spyware to load onto someone's phone or computer? I'm telling you, technology can be good and bad."

"Girl, I know," nodded Natalie, slowly chewing on a biscuit. "I'm just glad you were smart enough to do some research and you were careful. C'mon, let's go downtown and file a report and get a restraining order. It's time out for this madness. Ellis needs to be stopped once and for all."

You may try to keep your decision to leave the relationship a secret; however your friends and family will probably know very quickly. They already sense your unhappiness. They have seen the worried looks on your face, the mood swings, and the unexplained absences from important events. They also know when you are lying to cover up something you are embarrassed about. Those who know and love you cannot be kept out of this transition. In fact, you need them to help you through it, which is why you *must* level with them. You have to confess to them you are going through a period in your life that requires support and understanding.

God already knows your pain and worry. He will open doors for you and work on the internal processes of your survival; your friends and family can help with the day-to-day physical struggles. Let them know what you are doing and how you plan to accomplish it. Ask them to help you follow the rules outlined in the following chapters. Ask them to keep you from returning to the pain you need to leave behind, to give you honest advice, and invite you to join them in new activities. Ask them to make sure you are up on Sunday morning ready for worship. Finally, request that they regularly check on you to see if you need assistance or resources. Sometimes, a phone call from a trusted friend or loved one makes all the difference between a step forward and a step backward.

It is **highly** recommended that you talk to your pastor

and seek counseling during this period. The more support and prayer you can solicit from others, the better. We all know that prayer changes things, and you are in the midst of a total lifestyle change. You will need prayer and support to get through this period.

In addition to support, there is another reason for confession. When you confess your mistakes or struggles and declare to friends and family that you are starting a new life, you have a commitment they can examine. God examines your heart, but you need to be completely honest with others. Set a goal that your inner circle knows about so you are accountable to them and God. You are a role model, even if you don't know it. Make a public announcement and surround yourself with barriers to returning to the old life of abuse, making it difficult to turn back. Wrap your total being into this new existence with every ounce of energy and thought. This is a new opportunity to allow God to reshape you on the Potter's wheel. Virtues such as faith, honesty, credibility, generosity, and optimism can be molded into a clean heart. Only through complete commitment to a healthy new life will you succeed.

Let's not forget the children. How do you explain to them that their father is gone or why you are sad? A positive spin for children is always best. If the culprit is your husband and the father of your children, tell them that dad and mom need some time alone and things will be a little different for a while. Assure them that the separation is not their fault and is best for everyone. Assure them that everything will be fine but different, and that their dad will call them as soon as he can.

Children's lives should be structured with personalized time. With the move, their schedules will be disrupted and they may be in new surroundings. Insecurity of the unknown abounds in their heads. Keep your word so they know what to expect. If you say that Friday night is movie night, keep your promise. Children can motivate you to be your best—they are watching to see how you handle yourself and manage them.

Supplement their routines with new hobbies and people, and plan activities according to your budget. Riding bikes, playing board games, or taking walks in the park are inexpensive ways to occupy their time. Fill the void as much as you can with free or low-cost entertainment. Frugality may be the new normal. You are living on one income and a budget is a critical component of living day to day. You can invent special days for them to enjoy and celebrate. It's all about changing the environment in a pleasant way to help them blend the past into the future. If available and affordable, enroll the children in art classes, music lessons, or a sport activity. And each night before they go to bed, pray with them for peace and safety and thank God for the day.

Your children may also require counseling. Satan has a way of injecting himself into family problems and creating chaos among family members, even children. Immediately seek help if children are withdrawn or acting out. Experienced counselors can probe to expose the true feelings and issues in a child's fragile mind. Teenagers can be especially rebellious during a season of unpleasant change and stress. Counseling is absolutely the best way to address it, along with focused parental attention. Your children didn't create the abuse and separation, and they must be reassured of this fact. Refrain from any negative discussions about divorce, separation, or their father. Children must know they are safe, secure and loved, especially when the family structure has changed.

If your children are boys, they may especially miss their father's involvement. Boys may often take out their frustration with negative behaviors at home and school. Mentors or a male family member may help fill the void, but counseling is the best remedy for this problem.

Resist dating during your time of recovery. Do not think that a new boyfriend will ease the pain; you aren't ready. Bringing another male into the lives of your children, male or female, confuses and complicates the healing that must begin. Change is never easy when the family is broken. With time and concentrated prayer, God erases the scars of anger and disappointment. Time and faith heals all wounds.

Checklist on Protecting Yourself from Technology Abuse: Strategies for Safer Technology Use

Technology can be very helpful, but it can also be used to control or harm victims of domestic violence and stalking.

- **Use a computer that the abuser cannot access directly or remotely**, so your Internet use cannot be tracked or recorded. Consider using a computer in a public library, a trusted friend's house, or an Internet café.

- **Avoid using email** to talk to anyone about the danger or abuse in your life, because email is not always a safe or confidential way to communicate. Hotlines or crisis lines are a much safer way to talk about the abuse in your life.

- **Change passwords** of email and online accounts frequently. This may not be the safest option for everyone.

- **Install a firewall protection** such as ZoneAlarm (free at zonealarm.com) to guard against hackers. Be sure to physically disconnect your computer from the Internet whenever possible. Simply turning off your computer is not enough.

  - Firewall: A computer security system that prevents unwanted data or individuals from entering your computer undetected.

- **Limit your use of cordless phones** or baby monitors. Always switch to a corded telephone before exchanging sensitive information.

- **Check possible hiding places** for global positioning system (GPS) devices or chips, such as, car seats and trunks, under the hood of your car, jewelry, your purse, and cell phone.
- **Get a post office mailbox that is not close to your home** and use the address to fill out any applications that require personal information.
- **Ask where your personal information is stored**. Find out if your court system is publishing records on the Internet. Request that they seal your records or restrict who can access that information.
- Places that may have information about you:
  - Department of Motor Vehicles
  - Voter registration
  - Utility companies
  - Tax appraisals and real estate information
  - Grocery stores, video clubs, auto repair chains and other vendors
  - Academic/school records

Resources from the Ohio Domestic Violence Network

7

MOVING DAY

"God has not given us a spirit of fear, but of power, love and a sound mind" (2 Timothy 1:7).

*M*oving out on your own is a physical and emotional release. It's scary, unfamiliar, and at the same time, exciting. It requires concentrated planning. To do it well, timing is everything. When you are in crisis mode it can be hard to think logically and remember everything, so if at all possible, avoid moving out under duress. Here are some of the basics:

1. The library and the Internet contain unlimited information regarding local and national domestic violence information. So you are not tracked, use computers at work (unless you work for your abuser), the library, domestic violence shelters, or at a friend or family member's home. In short, use a computer that your abuser does not have access to. Request a new library card and assign a PIN other than the previous one. This ensures that your abuser cannot hack into your library account, determine the branch you visit, and when you are on a terminal.

2. Local domestic violence agencies have a plethora of resources and information to assist victims and their families. Keep in mind, the people who staff these agencies have already navigated the course you are

about to take. Heed their advice.

3. In a confidential place, store numbers for domestic violence agencies, the police, and shelters.

4. As you plan your move, begin gathering and storing records away from the house. Make copies of tax returns and all joint credit account statements. Get original birth certificates, social security cards, passports, and family records. Insurance and medical records are equally important. And don't forget any prescription medications for you and the children.

5. If you are married, immediately contact your bank and creditors to advise that you are in the process of a divorce or separation, and to alert you of any suspicious activity on your account. It is strongly recommended that you start a new banking relationship with a different financial institution.

6. If you are not married, any legal agreements should be severed, even if you must seek the counsel of an attorney. If you cannot afford an attorney, many areas provide Legal Aid for their residents.

7. So your mail is forwarded, **change your mailing address online, not in person at the post office**. The confirmation of the change of address will be emailed to you, therefore, have it sent to a new email address that your abuser cannot access. If you change your address in person, the post office will mail the confirmation to your home/old address, something you don't want as this will reveal your new address to your abuser. If you don't have a permanent address, the post office can hold your mail until you retrieve it.

8. Immediately inform close family and friends of the abuse and your plans to leave. This shouldn't be a surprise to them; usually they have already recognized signs of the abuse. It may be best if you can move in with a supportive family member or friend. Don't plan to stay there forever. Set a time frame to be in your own place. No matter how old you are, if you move

back home, you have to respect the rules of the house. This can be difficult for anyone.

9. Notify your children's school of your new address. If you move, this may mean changing school districts, something you must give much thought to and requires advance research. Your children may be involved in sports, cheer, dance, band and other school-related clubs that will keep them occupied during this time of transition. If your children are young, try to pack their favorite toy and books.

10. Communication is vital. Alert the school who is authorized to pick up the children. Talk to their teachers and explain the separation. Ask them to notify you of any changes in your children's behavior during this time of transition.

11. Notify your employer of the abuse through the company's Employee Assistance Plan. Your employer may have a protection plan in place to assist you. They may also be able to block phone from calls from your abuser and offer security escorts to walk you to your vehicle.

12. If you continue to use a cell phone that is part of a plan with your abuser, he can track you. There are several cell phone technologies that allow others to track locations, view text messages, and even listen in on conversations. Immediately change your phone number(s), but notify your family and loved ones of the changes. If possible, purchase a prepaid cell phone so your whereabouts cannot be tracked.

13. Remove important and shared emails, email contacts, phone numbers, etc. from the home computer. Close current email accounts and set up a new account with a new password. The new email account is needed for critical and necessary communication, such as the children's school. This can preclude your abuser from tracing you and diverting your accounts to his control.

14. It is important to create new passwords for online bill

pay, banking, social media and other transactions. Do not use passwords that can be easily guessed. Don't leave anything to chance. With today's technology, your abuser can acquire passwords using spyware or keylogging software. Avoid websites such as Facebook and LinkedIn or remove your profiles until your separation is final and you are safe.

15. Precious memories need not be lost in a separation. If possible, don't leave behind mementos, photos, valuables, antiques, or anything that means something to you. If time permits, and it doesn't alert your abuser of your desire to move out, transfer valuables or sacred items bit by bit. If and only if you have time, use a camera phone to take pictures of valuables you leave behind.

16. Begin the legal process of separation. Contact an attorney or Legal Aid for a consultation and explain all facets of the relationship and why you want out. This is very important if you fear bodily harm or have children and fear for their safety as well. A restraining order may be necessary for visitation arrangements with your children.

In spite of careful planning, the best plans can go awry. If your abuser is present when you move, or you fear he may show up, don't hesitate to immediately contact the authorities for protection.

Studies show that access to shelter services leads to a 60-70% reduction in incidence and severity of re-assault during the 3-12 months' follow-up period compared to women who did not access shelter. Shelter services led to greater reduction in severe re-assault than did seeking court or law enforcement protection, or moving to a new location. (Campbell, JC, PhD, RN, FAAN. Anna D. Wolf, Johns Hopkins University School of Nursing, Protective Action and Re-assault: Findings from the RAVE study.) Source: http://dvrc-or.org.

Month One

8

THE TWILIGHT ZONE

"Immediately the Spirit drove Him into the wilderness. And He was there in the wilderness forty days, tempted by Satan, and was with the wild beasts; and the angels ministered to him" (Mark 1:12).

The best way to describe the first day you leave an abusive relationship is similar to an episode that was broadcast years ago on *The Twilight Zone*. A young girl fell into the fourth dimension, a place and time that offered no familiar sights, sounds, or people. Stumbling onto the spot behind the wall in her home, she immediately knew it was unlike anything she had experienced in her brief life on earth. Everything was gray. There was no sky, land, or water. The sights and sounds were different and the familiar landmarks from her past had disappeared.

Peering in a mirror, she knew she was the same person, yet somehow she looked different. Scared, she wondered if she had changed inwardly. She didn't feel like the same person...it was as if something inside was surgically removed. She wasn't sure if it was day or night or if she was coming or going. There was nothing to lean on and she wasn't sure who she could depend on. The option to go back was not available, which forced her to explore her new surroundings in order to survive.

The first day you separate yourself from a painful relationship is a day of unfamiliar feelings and thoughts. It is your Twilight Zone—your personal season in the wilderness. Each time you think about the peace you seek, you notice the ache of not having the comfort of that voice, that face, the physical presence of your former loved one. You long to reach back to the past, but this is not an option. You cannot look back, because when you gaze back now, you might not feel the pain you felt the day before. It is hiding behind memories of happier days, when pleasure was greater than pain, and shades of gray were reserved for cloudy days.

This period of withdrawal is the hardest part of the journey. Take it one minute at a time, one hour, one day, and one long night at a time. Be assured that morning arrives with the fresh mercies of God. You may not be able to discern if you slept or if you are rested. Exhaustion gets up with you and wraps you like a winter coat. Although you feel tired, you can make it through the first day. This is a marathon, not a sprint.

> *"Through the Lord's mercies we are not consumed, because His compassions fail not. They are new every morning; great is your faithfulness. 'The Lord is my portion' says my soul, therefore I hope in Him" (Lamentations 3:22-24).*

The Month One marathon begins with the withdrawal phase, which eliminates any contact with your abuser. During this time, you will think someone added hours to the day and especially the night. It is a time of insecurity; when you pretend you are smiling when you aren't sure which emotion has kicked its way to the front of your heart. Like an out-of-body experience, you go through the motions in this wilderness. There are no familiar landmarks or benchmarks upon which you can rely. Tears are right behind your eyelids, so you must ask God for the eternal tissue to wipe them as they form. Everything feels surreal. Food doesn't taste the same and your regular habits are unfamiliar. You pretend to be normal, knowing all the while you are forever changed. Without formal training, you become an award-winning actress and continue to develop your character each day.

If possible, start the Month One marathon phase on a Sunday, not a holiday or birthday. It is even better if you start it after attending church, after asking God for strength, direction, and favor as you endure the temporary storm. The elements of this phase **must include** the following to produce a total lifestyle change.

1. If possible, eliminate all communication with your abuser. Do not call him, his friends, or family members unless there are children involved. You may need police involvement for safe transition of visitations. You do not need to be convinced to return to the relationship during this phase. Although some family members may attempt to patch up the relationship, you must get accustomed to not being a part of his world and begin creating your own. This is not the time for reconciliation.

2. Do not make any posts to social media such as Facebook, Twitter or Instagram that can reveal your whereabouts. Temporarily removing your profile is an option for consideration.

3. Make no physical contact, even if you must find a new place to live (THIS IS IMPERATIVE). Change your patterns. Get a restraining order if necessary. Don't go to places where you might run into your abuser. If you see him, walk the other way. If possible, avoid him if he tries to approach you. Immediately call security or the police if he persists.

4. Each time you think of your abuser, immediately begin to pray and ask God to redirect your thoughts to Christ and His power. If you can only repeat the Lord's Prayer, do that. It all works.

5. Ask your friends and family not to mention his name unless absolutely necessary or due to an emergency. Cut off the gossip by advising them that you are moving forward with your life. It may be hard to control your emotions, but you must try to always think positively and be grateful for what God has delivered you from.

6. Listen to positive messages in the car and at home. Take the romantic CDs out of your car and replace them with inspirational music, self-improvement discussions, or sermons from your favorite minister. This change will keep your mind occupied with positive or faith-filled messages as you drive back and forth to work and around town. Focus on your new life, not the life you are leaving behind.

7. Create a daily schedule to follow as closely as possible. Program each hour of the day with activities. Within the plan, include a diary of your thoughts and emotions and how you managed them. This helps you obtain balance and reminds you of what should be done each hour of the day to keep your life moving forward.

8. Do not resort to alcohol, or prescription or illegal drugs to calm your fears or anxiety. A false sense of comfort will only deepen your despair and create more problems that are difficult to resolve. Consult a doctor if you develop any new mental or physical health conditions.

Finally, remember that in spite of how isolated you feel you are not alone. God is with you. He is in your bedroom, in your car, at your desk, and even in the bathroom. He promises never to leave you, which means He always has your back and is creating the new life of peace He promised. He is your peace and your portion. More than a friend, He is your Father. He provides every resource and person you need, exactly when needed. You will emerge stronger, happier, and wiser.

NOTE: Ninety-two percent of women surveyed listed reducing domestic violence and sexual assault as their top concern. The Violence Against Women Act is successful legislation that has reduced domestic violence rates by fifty-eight percent since it was first passed in 1994. It was renewed in 2013. As reported by Ashley Parker, a Washington-based reporter for the *New York Times*, the newly passed legislation creates and expands federal programs to assist local communities with law enforcement and aiding victims of domestic and sexual abuse. The bill also offers protections for gay, bisexual, or transgender victims of domestic abuse. Additionally, it allows American Indian women who are assaulted on reservations by non-Indians to take their case to tribal courts, which otherwise would not have jurisdiction over assailants who do not live on tribal land. Source: www.nytimes.com, February 28, 2013.

9

ONE, TWO, BUCKLE MY SHOE

"Order my steps in thy word: and let not any iniquity have dominion over me" (Psalm 119:133).

Eva's life was a jigsaw puzzle with a million pieces that didn't seem to fit. She lost eight pounds in the first month of her separation and her clothes looked like they belonged to someone else. Due to the lack of sleep, she knew she must have looked tired most of the time. She *was* tired but she knew she had to keep moving during the day.

Eva felt like a robot, awakening each morning and doing everything by a script and a timeframe. Every moment was filled with an activity or errand and fatigue became her friend in the evening. *One two, buckle my shoe.* It was important to have a plan, a process, and a program to get through the day. A daily planner shouted her marching orders and a diary helped her record the high and low points of each day for future reference.

An idle mind is said to be the devil's workshop, and can be just that. During quiet moments, Eva's mind lingered in worry and sadness. She felt productive racing against the clock to get as many things completed by her self-imposed due dates. At times, she was so busy she actually forgot about her past as she became engaged in the present. Eva reminded herself daily, "God gave His best, so I must give my best."

The realization of her separation from Ellis draped Eva's heart like a thick wool blanket. During those times she chose not to think about a future as a single parent. She knew this would only set her back into worry wonderland and she certainly didn't want to go back there. She learned to freeze thoughts in her mind before they unfolded, pull out her "to do" list, and estimate when she would complete the tasks. Saturdays would roll something like this:

7:00	Out of bed. Prayer and a light breakfast while the girls slept.
7:30	Exercise. Walk thirty minutes with the dog around neighborhood.
8:30 -10:00	Prepare breakfast. Make plans for the day. Work on bills.
10:00-11:00	Clean the house.
11:00-12:00	Errands (cleaners, hair salon, etc.)
12:00-1:00	Library or park.
2:30-3:30	Grocery shopping.
3:30-5:00	Laundry and kids' homework.
5:00-6:00	Dinner
6:00-8:00	TV and plan for Sunday activities.
8:00 -10:00	Talk to family or friends via email or watch a DVD.
10:00-?	Bedtime with prayer and reflection, or reading.

It might be a while before you feel comfortable with your down time. Consider activities that bring you pleasure. Keep music, a book, a tablet, or a laptop on hand to keep your mind occupied. Engage yourself with crossword puzzles, word games, Sudoku, movies, board games, cards, or sewing; whatever you need to do to absorb your thoughts will help.

You may be invited to parties or dinner with friends, and if they can respect your circumstances, go. All too often *old* friends bring up *old* memories and *old* questions with *old* answers. You need to focus on the *new* you with your *new* life. If you don't feel comfortable socializing with friends, don't do it. Create your own memories and avoid backtracking to an unsettling past that makes you feel ill at ease. You will have enough time to deal with those feelings on your own, without the aid of others. This is your marathon and you must run it with the shoes that fit your feet now, not the ones you wore last year. Eventually, you will feel more comfortable in social settings.

10

2:00 A.M. TRAIN

"He will not allow your foot to be moved; He who keeps you will not slumber. Behold, He who keeps Israel shall neither slumber nor sleep" (Psalm 121:3, 4).

*J*oy didn't know when she finally fell asleep. Surfing the television channels for something interesting was futile; she couldn't find anything that suited her need for entertainment or relaxation. Frustrated, she gave up and ran a hot bath.

For some reason, she couldn't sit still in the tub and enjoy the warm bubbles as they danced around her body. Joy felt as if she were sitting in an unknown cave, defenseless and ill at ease. She quickly bathed and stepped out to try a glass of wine.

As she sat in bed, she realized it was two o'clock in the morning, leaving four hours before she had to be up and at it. Donovan would be waiting for her to fix breakfast and send him on his way, and once again she couldn't sleep. This was the third of such nights—insomnia was becoming a merry-go-round. As she thought about not falling asleep it became an obsession. It was as if Joy was under the control of some evil sleep monster who kept her keyed up and alert, when she needed to be tired and drowsy.

Sitting on the edge of the bed, Joy thought about how she could never control the temperature in her home when she was with Jonathan. She was constantly cold at night and awoke many mornings congested because of her allergies. Back then, she frequently returned to the dream of being single, when she could listen to quiet music and set the room temperature at seventy-three degrees, perfect for her sleep.

Admittedly, night was always problematical for Joy. She learned to sleep with one eye open when she was with Jonathan, in fear he would start an explosion over nothing. Even worse, she rarely slept soundly because she wanted to hear Donovan if he awakened during the night. Imagining the sun as a beacon for her future, Joy welcomed the first light of morning. Dawn introduced a fresh beginning, holding new opportunities for liberation from the nightmare of abuse.

Similar to an infant, it's normal to confuse days and nights. You are going through a life-changing experience and your body is running hard to keep up with your mind. Without proper rest, you may find yourself tired and almost falling asleep at work. Daydreaming while driving permits momentary escapes, but it is another form of distracted driving you must avoid. You lose concentration easily and struggle to get your mind back on track where it belongs. Your nerves are shot and you need to unwind the dense and familiar yarn of abuse that has wrapped itself around your thoughts and emotions.

When night falls and all is quiet, you toss and turn in a bed that doesn't feel like it's yours. Pillows are uncomfortable and your body cannot find the peace you need to sleep. The digital alarm clock screams at you: 2:00 a.m.! Is any of this familiar?

Nights are typically when you are most vulnerable to worry and anxiety. It is the time when your head fills with numerous questions and thoughts. It is when the sights and sounds of pain and loneliness creep into your room. You long for an embrace, while knowing you can't allow that train of thought to continue.

It's a dead end with the person you left. Therefore, stop worrying if you made the right decision. Cease from wondering what he is doing and who he is with. And please don't set aside your dignity by conducting drive-bys, calling, or texting your abuser. You are a woman of worth and there is absolutely no stalking. You must not call his friends or family to discuss the separation or find out if they have heard anything. Stop this train! It goes nowhere. You made the commitment to turn away from abuse, so now walk the journey to the point where you are in control. You're not there yet. You're just beginning and this could be a rough ride.

How can you keep up this pace? It is imperative to be alert in the morning and arrive at work on time. What is the best way to keep the evil spirits of the past out of your mind, and to prevent negative thoughts and worries from climbing into your bed each night? Is it a glass of wine, a sleeping pill, or watching television? Drugs and alcohol are not safe solutions and can place you on a path to addiction and self-destruction.

The answer is a friend called Christ Jesus. He never sleeps. He is right there in the room with you, waiting for you to acknowledge His presence and calm down. Think about it...when was the last time you spent time communicating with Him, writing down your thoughts and listening for His voice to respond to your questions, needs, and desires?

When you recognize you are not alone, you can begin to accept your aloneness without being lonely. There is a difference. Loneliness has little to do with having a companion or husband. You can be lonely with a companion in the bed right next to you, snoring up a storm. Think of the night as the bridge to a new and better day. You can't get to tomorrow until you pass through the night.

So what else can you do to regain normal sleeping patterns? Let's assume the television, warm milk, and counting sheep hasn't worked.

Avoid caffeine after noon, and try chamomile tea in the evening. Don't take a nap after work. Instead get an exercise DVD, or find an inexpensive exercise class at a recreation center. One hour before your normal bedtime, take a warm bath. Read God's Word or something pleasant while soaking in the tub or sitting in a comfortable position. After you have prayed and meditated on His Word, thank God for another day and ask for a good night's sleep (Psalm 3:5, Psalm 4:8, Proverbs 3:24). You can also try the following:

1. Fill your mind with pleasant and peaceful thoughts and ideas. Play soft music or an inspirational CD.
2. Try to say Psalm 23 from beginning to end over and over in your mind. Imagine each verse as you say it, and place yourself in the vision you create.
3. If darkness bothers you, purchase a night light for comfort.
4. If the radio or music keeps you awake, try a fan. The sound of a fan is calming to many and can help you fall asleep within a few minutes. There are also great sound machines that remind you of an ocean or a waterfall.
5. Do not go to the computer. A few minutes on the computer can turn into hours and before you realize it, you miss out on much needed sleep.

Should the 2:00 a.m. wakeup call come again, there are natural sleep aids such as Melatonin that work for many people. If falling asleep is a regular problem, consult your physician for other remedies. There are many strategies to assist you in returning to a normal sleep pattern, while reviving and rejuvenating your body. Try these methods every night until you look forward to bedtime as the time to unwind and gear up for the morning's new challenges.

Pssst! Did you think we forgot to mention the "S" word? If we didn't bring it up, you might wonder if we know what we are talking about. Sex is a normal part of a marital relationship and for many, an important one. Right now, however, this is a subject that must be put on the shelf until you get through the detox phase and perhaps some time after that.

Vulnerable, you are not ready for an intimate relationship with anyone—you are held together with duct tape and safety pins. All you need is for someone to pick up your crystal soul and smash it on the pavement. When you haven't ironed the wrinkles out of the sheets you just left, you need not add more. Additionally, physical intimacy doesn't mean love is guaranteed or even present. When a godly love isn't present, sex is nothing more than short-term gratification. God fashioned sex for the covenant of marriage, not singlehood. It is important to love yourself as God's daughter, fashioned for His glory and fit for His use.

Dating at this point is not recommended as it can be a distraction. A new relationship can impede the development of your one-on-one relationship with God. It can also prevent you from knowing how to be content in whatever situation you are in, single or married. It may not feel like it, but this is the best possible place you can be. Platonic male friends are fine, especially if they are longtime friends; however, be careful not to confuse support with affection. And remember, weeping may endure for the night, but joy comes in the morning.

More importantly, give your emotional wounds time and attention to heal. Those wounds cannot heal with layers of worry and fear. They can heal with prayer, rest, and emotional fertilizer; the nourishment that comes from making the most of your time, talents, and treasures. Another relationship won't cure the pain from the past, so take time to know yourself, inside and out, as God's perfect design.

Let's repeat: **NO SEXUAL CONTACT OF ANY KIND. Total recovery from the abusive relationship is imperative. When you enter into a covenant of marriage based upon love, respect, commitment and the Word of God, you can appreciate and receive the blessings of intimacy.**

11

MIRROR, MIRROR

"I will praise You, for I am fearfully and wonderfully made; Marvelous are Your works, And that my soul knows very well" (Psalm 139:13-15).

Everyone called Joy "kitten" as a child. She had beautiful hazel eyes, dimpled cheeks, and soft black hair that cradled her face like a picture frame. She had grown to be a beautiful woman, in spite of a few extra pounds around her waist from the pregnancy. Her teeth were chipped in the front and she smiled with a slant to cover a broken tooth on the left side. Joy had not been to a professional beautician in months, and her hair was graying and broken off in several places. Her nails were short and neat, but she seldom found the time to apply polish. These days, a little lip gloss was all she added to her natural but neglected beauty.

Because she chose classic cuts, Joy was able to wear the same suits to work she had worn for years since Jonathan claimed she didn't need a new wardrobe. She enjoyed reading Oprah's magazine and imagining that she was one of the beautiful images advertising makeup or the latest fashion trends. Despite her best efforts, Joy disliked the way she looked and knew it was time to initiate an *extreme makeover*. At 45, she was at a crossroad, knowing if changes needed to be made, the time was now.

Her turbulent marriage forced Joy to sacrifice her appearance so much so that she avoided looking in the mirror. The mirror revealed the pain of abuse, the loss of self-esteem, and fear of her future. The scar on her cheek from a previous assault was almost faded. It served its purpose as a constant reminder of her journey from pain to promise. When she was with Jonathon, makeup served as a valuable concealer each morning to cover bruises or tired eyes. Sometimes she didn't remember how she arrived at work in the morning; her mind drifted aimlessly as she navigated the path to her office. Once, she unknowingly showed up wearing two completely different shoes. Her assistant knew the stress she was under and pulled her aside to whisper, "maybe you need to go and look in the mirror before you take your first appointment."

Thank God for the friend who loved her enough to tell her the truth! Sister-friends are essential to maintaining a journey to fulfillment. Joy didn't need any more drama in her life, especially at work. Gossip was already circulating about her marriage and she didn't want it to impact her performance or the relationship with her executive vice president.

Once Joy gathered the courage to leave Jonathan, she desperately wanted a new image, a new smile, and a new life. With a new sense of freedom as well as control, she made a list of daily activities she could afford and perform before or after work, without interrupting Donovan's activities. She dedicated a half-hour before work and a half-hour after work to her new and improved image each week for three months. Goals included regular exercise, healthier food choices, adding a few affordable pieces to her wardrobe each month, and definitely a visit to the dentist, OB/GYN, and her family doctor. She noticed she was having trouble reading small print, and made an appointment with an optometrist. Fortunately, she squeezed one hundred dollars from her check each month for her self-improvement fund.

In time, physical improvements helped Joy to see her God-given beauty. Unfortunately, the emotional scars remained etched in her heart and burned in her mind. She knew she would have to work on the inside as well as the outside to become whole again. After talking to her pastor and Aminah, she joined a support group of women who had been abused or violated from domestic violence.

Joy dreaded questions about Jonathan and chose to simply tell the truth. When friends, coworkers, and family asked about him, she simply replied, "We are no longer together." As the separation turned from days to weeks, her fear of ever trusting another man was a top priority after reclaiming her own self-worth. Joy didn't want to stay single forever, but knew she had to shut the door to the past and launch a new life on her own.

As you transition through the first month of your new life, you might need to "fake it until you make it." Pretend you feel great, look great, and have everything under control–until you do. It's okay to feign happiness even if you aren't happy. Constantly reminding yourself of future possibilities and reciting positive affirmations and scriptures will transform pretense into reality. Happiness will follow.

A checklist for re-inventing yourself is below. Each step can become part of your daily routine, and in a few days, you will feel better mentally and physically.

1. Pray before getting out of bed. Thank God for rest and another day. Thank God for your family and your job, and honor Him for providing you with unique blessings and gifts. Say it out loud so you can hear yourself. Ask Him to give you the strength to make the most of this day, to give you pleasant things to say, and allow you to handle each hour in a peaceful manner. Ask Him to give you the resources to bless

and help others, and to mold you into the woman He destined you to be. And finally, ask Him to keep you and your family free from evil of any kind.

2. Exercise for twenty to thirty minutes while listening to the news. The news keeps you informed about the world around you and helps you ignore the movement of your feet on a treadmill, elliptical or walking in place. Free weights can be added to strengthen your upper body. You can also exercise to a DVD or a downloaded program. Music is great for walking in rhythm and passing time quickly. Pick up the pace at the beginning of each week.

3. Choose your wardrobe weekly and iron clothes the night before if they are wrinkled. Check them in direct sunlight for spots, rips, or missing buttons. Always look your best because unfortunately, people judge you by your external presentation. If funds are tight and a new wardrobe is needed, there are local agencies that assist women in transition with a new wardrobe, such as the organization Dress for Success.

4. If there are clothes in your closet that remind you of the person you are leaving behind, give them to a women's charity or social service agency. Clothes carry memories too, and you must stay away from anything that binds you to the past. If funds permit, get a few classic pieces that reflect the current styles or the new you. Change is good and the pieces you put together could be different colors or styles. Classic work wardrobes include a basic black, navy or gray suit, and white blouses and black pumps. Alternate blouse colors or pair different tops with suits for a fresh look. Check out consignment stores or thrift shops for inexpensive additions or accessories. The same suit can gain new life with a different top or necklace.

5. Polish your shoes. Keep an instant shine sponge near your shoes to wipe them before you rush out

the door. When the heels are worn, replace the shoes or repair the heels; this is more cost effective if the shoes are in good shape.

6. Your hair is important and should be healthy and manageable. Studies show that stress causes hair breakage, so keep the tresses trimmed. Although gray can be distinguished on many women, it requires special care. Color is exciting and can bring new life to your total image. Within your budget, visit a stylist on a regular basis to keep your hair attractive and healthy. Request a new look if you are unhappy with your current appearance. You can also visit a beauty school that provides student services at reduced rates.

7. Maintain your skin by keeping it clean and moisturized. If you are under stress your complexion can be more sensitive. Some scars can be minimized with the help of a good esthetician, and if you can afford it, a facial now and then will greatly improve your complexion and the condition of your skin. The aging process comes with special skin challenges. Ask friends to recommend over-the-counter products if a professional visit is not in the budget.

8. Makeup can make or break your image. Too much gives a false image and too little will not add to your best features. Drop by a department store and ask for a makeup demonstration at one of the counters. Use the tips gathered from the demo to create your own, less expensive routine. If it takes longer than seven minutes, it may be too much. Use makeup that is colorful but not overdone; look vibrant but not painted.

9. Nails should be manicured weekly. Hands are clear expressions of your emotional health, and the texture and length of your nails can communicate stress or confidence.

10. Jewelry is a refreshing addition to classic dresses and

suits. Pearls, gold, or silver work for office attire and color can be added to evenings or special occasions. Contemporary jewelry can also help women to develop a stylish flair. A good rule of thumb is not more than four pieces per outfit, including earrings, necklace, a watch, and a bracelet or pin.

11. Begin an eating plan that includes protein, vegetables, and fruits as a foundation for each meal. Limit carbohydrates and fats as much as possible and increase water intake to at least eight glasses per day. This plan will also improve your children's eating habits as you reduce the reliance on fast foods and unhealthy snacks. An inexpensive tool for weight management is a cell phone app that measures calories and exercise when joining a gym or professional diet club isn't possible.

12. A massage every once in a while is a great stress reliever.

13. Keep an extra pair of shoes, earrings, hose, and some cologne in your desk drawer. Stuff happens at work, too.

Work hard to reinvent yourself; you didn't get tired overnight. Prayer, diet, exercise, hair and skin care, support groups, counseling, and recreational activities are all part of the package. What is it you want to accomplish during the next ninety days? Take a picture of yourself in Month One and at the end of Month Three. Note the changes and the progress you make each week.

The best investment you can make in your recovery is to find something that makes you feel good, something that makes you laugh. You are important. Reading the Scriptures will bring joy and strength. Attending an aerobics or line dance class is great exercise. Gardening connects you to nature and the majesty of God. Seek those activities and people that affirm or validate your importance and peace.

If you aren't used to being alone, learn to be by yourself.

If no one else is there, God is with you. When you are by yourself, it's easier to hear God's personal message to you. His voice can come by way of the sun shining through the clouds, a fresh breeze across your face, or a rainbow in the sky. In His earthly kingdom and His heavenly kingdom there is glory, majesty, joy and peace. Quiet time to collect your thoughts gives you the opportunity to receive divine strategies from God and to set your priorities on how to move forward, especially if you are in the midst of legal matters. And by the way, it's okay to talk to yourself. When you hear your own voice affirming how great you are, you will eventually agree with what you hear. Amen!

Lasting change doesn't happen overnight. The investments you make today in your physical, spiritual, and emotional health will reap future benefits.

Month Two

12

REMNANTS OF A RELATIONSHIP

"He who dwells in the secret place of the Most High shall abide under the shadow of the Almighty. I will say of the Lord, "He is my refuge and my fortress; My God, in Him I will trust" (Psalm 91:1, 2).

*T*urning the sharp corner into the elementary school parking lot, Kaitlyn exhaled. It was good to be back to work. She was anxious to see her fourth graders and begin a new art project this quarter. Working with clay and paint was therapy for her, something their innocent minds couldn't grasp. Kaitlyn was sure that somewhere in that bunch was another Ernie Barnes, another Georgia O'Keeffe, another Lisa Cliff, another Elizabeth Catlett Mora, or another Picasso. The familiar smell of her art room enveloped her and she set her iPod to listen to Adele and Joss Stone. Here she was at home, just like the small studio in the house she rented with her brother.

Two years had passed and Kaitlyn was without a man in her life. This was exactly the way she wanted it, at least for now. A striking blond, Kaitlyn accepted a few dinner dates here and there, but she wasn't emotionally prepared to share her heart. After leaving Brandon, she couldn't trust herself to remain in a committed relationship. Perhaps in time she would be set free of the scars—scars of a relationship that was ultimately not meant to be.

Coming from a home where she witnessed abuse, Kaitlyn

was certain it would never happen to her. If anyone could spot an abuser a mile down a dirt road it was Kaitlyn. In spite of the violence her stepfather exhibited, she was fortunate to be raised around two-parent families, watching men who were good providers love and care for their families. She frequently wondered if God would ration some portion of that same bliss to her.

In her eyes, Brandon was her portion, her prince, her knight in shining armor. He was charming, good looking, and had a savoir faire that immediately attracted Kaitlyn. A former Marine who had recently returned from two tours of duty, Brandon loved adventure. Soon after meeting, he and Kaitlyn spent every free moment together. It wasn't long before Kaitlyn began leafing through bridal magazines at checkout counters and imagining places to honeymoon. She became enchanted with the idea of being Mrs. Brandon Scott.

Time reveals all secrets, mysteries, and skeletons in the closet. It releases the hidden demons that lie dormant. Within a year of dating, the bad boy in Brandon emerged. His sudden bursts of temper and mood swings became more frequent and his compliments turned to criticism. Kaitlyn suspected Brandon was bipolar, and began feeling uncomfortable with the derogatory comments and mean jokes about women. Even worse was the amount of time he spent on the computer late into the evening. Brandon was extremely secretive about his surfing, which raised Kaitlyn's suspicions about the websites he visited.

The first dose of reality came when Brandon pulled her hair when she resisted his sexual overtures while she was reviewing student assignments. She eventually gave in to avoid further abuse, but to her it was rape, not consensual sex. When he realized her reaction, Brandon's apologies flowed with the obligatory promises to never do it again.

The second incident of abuse sent Kaitlyn running from their townhouse and hiding behind a dumpster not far from their building. Kaitlyn could hear Brandon calling as she crouched in fear. She waited until dawn to creep back inside. Appearing humble and contrite for his brash temper, Brandon promised to get help. "I don't think I can live without you, Kait," he whispered as small tears trickled down his face.

Deep within, Kaitlyn realized Brandon's behavior was turning increasingly erratic and their relationship was becoming more dangerous for her. It reminded her of the abuse her mother suffered at the hands of her stepfather, which escalated year after year. The respect Kaitlyn held for Brandon diminished over the months and she no longer desired the intimacy of his arms. She saw his hands as formidable weapons, not conduits for caressing and holding. Uneasiness cloaked her like an early morning fog, shadowing her most nights and into the early morning hours.

It wasn't long before Kaitlyn created an immediate plan to unravel her life with Brandon without incurring more harm and with little incident. She certainly didn't need him showing up at school, embarrassing her in front of her colleagues and frightening the students. She kept a spare set of car keys hidden outside their townhouse and always made sure the gas tank was full in case she suddenly needed to leave the apartment complex.

Within six weeks, Kaitlyn rented a small home across town with her brother. They moved her belongings while Brandon worked an overtime shift. She stopped mail delivery to the townhouse and rented a post office box as a precaution. As Kaitlyn hoisted boxes into the rented U-Haul truck, she knew that she never should have moved in with Brandon in the first place. What was she thinking? Unfortunately, enchantment took over common sense and good judgment. If her grandmother was alive she would have had a fit and scolded Kaitlyn for making a terrible choice. Her friends would have told her to run a "50"— a background check. The report would have revealed his conviction for assault against a former girlfriend. Kaitlyn soon realized she had taken a foolish chance not sharing the abuse, taking pictures, or contacting the police or a domestic violence agency earlier in the relationship. She was in harm's way and needed to get out.

Taking one last look at their apartment, Kaitlyn placed a note on the kitchen counter, warning Brandon that she was going to file a restraining order and that family and coworkers were alerted to his behavior. She wished him the peace he desperately needed, advised him to seek professional counseling, and asked him to respect her decision to end the relationship.

Her efforts to quietly move on were met with resistance. True to his forceful nature, Brandon ignored her requests and made attempts to jump-start the relationship. After several emails to her school account and texts that went unanswered, he waited in the school parking lot for Kaitlyn to emerge from a long day of teaching and staff meetings about the upcoming school year. She had to admit the man knew how to clean it up. Brandon was back to his handsome, debonair profile and boy did he smell good. Kaitlyn held her breath along with the fear that endeavored to grip her heart. She had mentally prepared for this moment and was not to be persuaded to give in and give him another try.

"Baby, I want us to start all over," Brandon begged. "I'm a changed man and my life is not the same without you. I'm taking anger management classes again and this time I'll see them through. I promise."

"Brandon, you've started those classes twice only to abandon them because you were bored," said Kaitlyn, the skepticism showing in her voice. "The only person in this relationship who has changed is me. I'm not the same woman you met a year-and-a-half ago. I'll never be the same and I'm never coming back. I'm done."

People who aren't set free from their sins and bad habits are prone to repeat them and such was Brandon's story. As Kaitlyn turned to walk away, Brandon grabbed her arm and yanked her to his chest. His eyes changed and immediately Kaitlyn sensed that violence was about to erupt. She had watched and starred in this movie before.

"Don't you dare leave me like this Kait; I'm the best thing that ever happened to you. You know you want me. Who do you think you are, anyway? You can't make it without me."

Kaitlyn's heart pounded and her head began to throb. Wrenching herself from Brandon's grip, she tried to slip between two cars and run. Her only safety was the school and the nearest door was at least forty yards away. Brandon yanked her back and pushed her face into a van window, pressing his frame against her back. Before she could scream, she was suddenly released from the side of the van. Out of the corner of her eye she saw a tall figure knock Brandon to the ground with the force of a professional boxer. It was old Jake, the school janitor.

Jake had cleaned the building for the past four years after retiring from serving as a pastor at a small church. He received a pension, but the part-time janitorial job kept him busy in the evenings, when he was especially lonely. He kept the school immaculate and was a reliable, quiet fixture. No one knew much about him except that he lost a teenage daughter six years ago to abuse. The pain of seeing his daughter Sophia's beautiful face beaten to a pulp continued to haunt him.

Jake's wife of twelve years died of leukemia, leaving him to raise their daughter, Sophia, alone. After her death, Jake continued in his role as pastor. With the support of a few close parishioners, he raised Sophia with lots of love and a firm hand. Jake's desire to protect Sophia and keep her close to him led her to rebel against his strict curfews and old-fashioned views on dating.

Everyone knew she was a "PK," a preacher's kid, and Sophia hated the label, the taunts and the teasing. She longed to be free and live the life of the wild bunch at school. The attempts to be free of her father's rules and his calling led Sophia to run with the wrong crowd. Despite Jake's best efforts, Sophia was fearless and it wasn't long before her outward show of independence attracted someone with a rebellious nature. The minute Jake met him at the front door, he knew Wade was trouble and he soon discovered that no amount of parenting could make Sophia think otherwise. What he didn't realize was that Sophia had low self-esteem and needed a mother figure or a strong female in her life. In her mind, Jake was dictatorial and she resented him and what he stood for. She latched onto Wade and quickly made one poor choice after another.

Within weeks of dating, Sophia was hanging on Wade and following behind him after school and sporting events. Her self-esteem was tied to Wade's reputation and the characteristic adolescent need to be popular. Sophia didn't see her inward and outward beauty; she only felt Wade's muscular arm around her waist and the looks of approval from her girlfriends. To her detriment, she ignored the warning signals that went off in her head and succumbed to Wade's pressure for sex. After all, he said he loved her and they were going to make a life together after graduation.

When Sophia became pregnant, Wade's treatment of her worsened as his resentment grew. Fatherhood was definitely not in his plans and he began to drink. Fearing her father's disappointment, Sophia kept the pregnancy a secret. She also covered up the bruises on her arms as the fights with Wade turned more and more violent.

Wade's drinking, anger, and unfaithfulness were more than Sophia was equipped to handle. One Friday night after a home game, they argued under the bleachers about the pregnancy and the rumors circulating around school about his new love interest, a sophomore cheerleader. Wade had been drinking—mixing alcohol with pills—and was pretty amped by the time the game ended. As the argument intensified, so did Wade's anger. He wanted to be free of Sophia and the pregnancy that was about to burden him with financial and parenting commitments he refused to accept. Wade felt trapped. When Sophia grabbed his arm as he turned to leave, he swung and landed a blow to her face. The second and third blows to her face forced her backwards, and she hit her head against a steel post. As she fell to the concrete, her last memory was the look of hatred on Wade's face. Sophia never regained consciousness and Jake didn't have the chance to say goodbye.

Still waters run deep and Jake's quiet nature was merely the surface of a man who had suffered much loss. Since that evening when he was called to the hospital, Jake's craggy face rarely smiled. He deeply mourned his wife and Sophia.

Sensing she was troubled, Jake spent extra time cleaning Kaitlyn's classroom and watched out for her after school. In some strange and calming way, her blonde hair and green eyes reminded him of the daughter he lost years ago.

"Call the authorities young lady and make sure you press charges against this sorry coward for assault," Jake advised her as Brandon staggered to his feet. "I'll be a witness if you need one."

Kaitlyn knew a record of the abuse needed to be on file. The time had come to take back her power and use the legal resources available to her. After making a police report and taking photos of her face, neck and arm, she drove home drenched in tears. Brandon's pursuit was beyond the passion of spurned love. It was madness, and if she didn't take measures to protect herself, she feared the violence would escalate into something beyond ugly.

What if Jake hadn't showed up? And, what does God do with monsters and the mentally ill, she wondered as she drew herself a warm bath. How do you rationalize with someone who isn't rational? Tossing their relationship over and over in her mind, Kaitlyn realized her knight in shining armor was simply a heartless tin man who lacked the courage to deal with his demons.

Fortunately, none of the students were present to witness the incident. At the sound of the bell, they had sprinted to humming school buses and parents who patiently waited for them to collect homework-filled backpacks. The next day, Kaitlyn covered the discoloration on her face with makeup and wore long sleeves to hide the purple bruises that marred her pale skin. It was unseasonably hot—eighty-five degrees—but she didn't care. She met with her principal after school and shared the incident and the status of her relationship with Brandon. Without a moment's hesitation, the principal contacted the school district's human resource office and put Kaitlyn in touch with an employee relations representative who assisted her with additional community resources.

From that day, Jake quietly made his presence known to Kaitlyn after school. Pushing the dust broom and with a slight nod of his balding head, he assured Kaitlyn he had her back without uttering a single word. From the first grade classroom window he watched her walk to her car, and when winter came he often cleaned her windshields as soon as he thought no one was looking.

Kaitlyn ended the school year by placing a neatly wrapped package inside the janitor's closest. It was one of her latest and, in her opinion, best paintings. She felt it was the most heartfelt way to say thank you to a true knight in shining armor.

One in five teens in a serious relationship reports having been hit, slapped, or pushed by a partner. Fourteen percent of teens report their boyfriend or girlfriend threatened to harm them or themselves to avoid a breakup. Many studies indicate that as a dating relationship becomes more serious, the potential for and nature of violent behavior also escalates. (Information provided by Oregon Law Center)

Teen Violence - Emotional Abuse Checklist
for Dating Violence

Check the answer that best fits your relationship	Often	Sometimes	Rarely	Never
Are your activities and interests looked upon as unimportant and trivial?				
Are you expected to drop what you're doing to meet your partner's needs?				
Do you have to account for all your time?				
Does your partner make light of important subjects saying things like, "Can't you take a joke?"				
Does your partner insist that everything is your fault?				
Do you have to ask permission to see or spend time with friends or family?				
Does your partner use violence or threats during an argument?				
Does your partner tell you nobody else would ever want you?				
Does your partner threaten to hurt her- or himself if you were to leave or break-up with them?				
Does your partner go through your personal things (locker, purse, notebooks, etc.) without permission?				
Are you afraid to talk about certain subjects unless your partner is in a good mood?				
Are you often accused of cheating on your partner or flirting with others, even though you are not doing these things?				
Does your partner humiliate or embarrass you in public?				

Does your partner use information you've confided in him or her against you?				
Does your partner compare you negatively to others?				
Does your partner use "guilt trips" to manipulate you?				
Does your partner make you feel obligated to be sexual in order for her/him to feel loved?				
Does your partner put you down about the way you look or dress?				
Does your partner make rules about what you can or cannot do?				

Source: Love is Not Abuse

13

24-7

"I will bless the LORD at all times; His praise shall continually be in my mouth" (Psalm 34:1).

Eva dropped Camille and Cara at latchkey about an hour before her day began. They quickly adapted to their new routines without Ellis and enjoyed the mornings. During the fifteen-minute drive, they talked in the car about their new life, what they would prepare for dinner, and planned special activities for the weekend. After several kisses goodbye, Eva frequently used the extra time to visit Barbara, a friend who was battling breast cancer. Barbara lived near the twins' school and Eva wanted her to know she was praying for her complete recovery. It also gave her time to spend with an essential person in her life. Barbara was a survivor and had overcome challenges not just with her physical health, but with a demanding job and a wayward son. She clung to a positive philosophy about life that Eva vitally needed as she began to reconstruct her own world. Eva needed Barbara as much as Barbara relied on Eva.

The women shared a cup of tea and talked about their children. Eva was extra careful not to complain about her separation from Ellis. Her problems seemed insignificant compared to Barbara's. Barbara was weak most days, but on occasion found excitement about the good news from the doctor's visit the day before. She was Eva's age, but the effects of the chemotherapy had destroyed her beautiful hair and caused her skin to look ashen and dull. In spite of her illness, Barbara was Eva's yardstick, helping her to measure her blessings and be grateful for health and family.

So she could be upbeat and positive, Eva quietly prayed before she entered Barbara's home. Barbara never complained about her circumstances and always reassured Eva that God was working on miracles for both of them. Upon leaving, she thanked God for the unexpected messages He always sent through Barbara, providing her with healing and strength to push forward during her transition. She ended each visit with a joke and a hug.

As you get accustomed to independence you must increase reliance on your best friend, Jesus, 24-7, all day. Wherever there is a void, you must praise Him, pray to Him, and practice His teachings—24-7.

Of course, it's always easy to be good when you are feeling good. But it's hard to *be good* when you feel down or depressed. By the second month, you feel a major emptiness in your life, and you still aren't used to the new routine. You know what your pattern is, although the passion in the movement may not be there. You aren't enthusiastic about going to work or doing the laundry, but you know you have to perform.

Here is an example of how to use the "Three Ps" 24/7:

1. **Pray:** When you awake get down on your knees. Ask God to allow you to be a better servant and reflection of His love.

2. **Praise:** Play inspirational music in your car that reminds you of how blessed you are in spite of

your loneliness. Thank Him for the small blessings you normally take for granted. Exercise to lively worship music and get fit in mind and body.

3. **Practice** His teachings: Say something pleasant to everyone you meet, even if it is just "good morning" or "isn't it a beautiful day?" It may seem awkward at first, but it really does bring a smile to most people, which can make you feel better.

4. **Pray**: Before a major decision or a potential conflict, say a prayer for tact and wisdom. Ask God to give you the right thoughts, words, and actions to act as He wants. Pray for your abuser, particularly that he seeks and receives sound counseling.

5. **Praise**: On your way home reflect on the ups and down of the day and how you handled them. Thank God for His patience and guidance throughout the day.

6. **Practice**: Demonstrate your faith by assuring your loved ones that everything is all right and there is nothing to worry about.

Now, even if you know you are acting, try to keep it going. Some days will be easier than others. Eventually joy will triumph over sadness. Your family and friends will respect your positive attitude and return the much needed love and affection.

At the end of your day, take extended time to pray for another day. Can you thank God for health, family, and provision? Can you thank Him for His protection and love? What about your job? Many people are unemployed. God even sneaks in special treats like the parking space closest to the office when rain is pouring down. Can you ask Him for rest and the opportunity to pray, praise, and practice His teachings one more day? Just think about what could have happened to you that God didn't allow. You were saved by His love and grace. How can you demonstrate your faith in action?

14

DRAMA DETOX

"The righteous should choose friends carefully, for the way of the wicked leads them astray" (Proverbs 12:26).

Fighting mild depression after her breakup with Brandon, Kaitlyn made it a personal goal to remain positive each day. Despite her best efforts, she noticed certain people in her circle did their level best to bring her down with their problems. Inconsiderate haters, she thought. Some of them knew she was stressed, but face it, misery loves company. Friends, family members, and coworkers would stop by and simultaneously drop some worrisome issue in her lap that didn't belong there. Kaitlyn didn't solicit the problems. A simple, "How are you doing today?" cranked their engines.

That's when the drama unfolded. Kaitlyn discovered that a fellow teacher was a closet alcoholic and Carl, the math teacher, constantly complained about mutual friends when they were in the teachers' lounge. Kaitlyn couldn't bear a whiney man, and Carl was whiney, continually complaining about some imaginary form of maltreatment. Cousin Mattie always wanted to borrow money she couldn't repay, and other family members found it their duty to inform her about Brandon and whom he was dating. On several occasions, Marcie, who was recently divorced, tried to drag Kaitlyn to her favorite club for a night on the town of dancing and flirting. With family and friends like these, Kaitlyn didn't need adversaries.

Kaitlyn realized she wasn't strong enough to shoulder their burdens and lifestyles along with her own. Since leaving Brandon, she decided to seek counseling to understand how she, of all people, fell into an abusive relationship. On one visit, the topic of her circle of support came up.

"To be honest, I want to divorce some folks who are really giving me the blues," Kaitlyn confided. "It seems I'm the confidante value meal for everyone around me. What should I do to get rid of them? They're like gnats swarming around my head—I want to swat them and make them go away."

"Make a list of all the people who are regulars in your life and decide if they are plusses or minuses," her counselor advised. "In no time, you'll be able to decide who needs to be swatted and who you should keep."

To detox the drama kings and queens in her life, he advised Kaitlyn to ask herself:

1. Do I need this person, and if so, why?
2. Do I feel better or worse after being with them?
3. Do they bring anything positive to my life or do they bring me down?
4. What are the ties that bind the relationship?
5. Am I afraid of ending the relationship? If so, why?
6. What method would I use to excuse myself from their lives without a major confrontation?

Kaitlyn returned home from counseling and sitting down with a cup of chai latte she decided to immediately make her list. She chose seven people who made the Drama Detox Most Wanted list. Several people in her life were perpetual gnats. They regularly swarmed her like a trash can, depositing their rubbish in her mind and leaving it there to ferment. Kaitlyn was determined to take action, just as she did when she chose to leave Brandon. Enough was enough.

After saving her list, she talked to her counselor before putting the plan into action. He warned that there would be some minor pain or discomfort, but this detox would be nothing like the withdrawal from Brandon. It was an exercise in life that would be useful again and again. Drama detox in motion!

With love and the gentlest of care, Kaitlyn diplomatically confronted the closet alcoholic and recommended the district's Employee Assistance Program for abuse counseling after he admitted to the habit. She advised Carl that she wasn't interested in tearing down her coworkers and spent less time in the teachers' lounge. Kaitlyn adeptly avoided her neighbor across the street by always being too busy to talk, and told Cousin Mattie she had no money in her budget for loans of any sort. She made sure word got around to the family by way of Aunt Ida that she was not the least bit interested in Brandon's life. Finally, she referred two church buddies to the pastor for assistance she was not qualified to offer. Marcie was a bit more difficult. She stopped returning her calls and when they ran into each other at a friend's graduation, Kaitlyn shared her discomfort with the singles' scene. Eventually, Kaitlyn detoxed her Most Wanted List out of her life during a period of several weeks and was grateful to her counselor for the sound advice. She was starting her new life with a clean slate, and learning to surround herself with positive people and positive thoughts.

And Another Thing: Family members can be the most difficult to confront because you love them and you know they love you. However, they may not know the dynamics of your situation as well as you, legally, emotionally, or spiritually. In love, they should be told that when you need advice you will seek it. They can be supportive, but take care that you don't allow them to insert themselves in your plans and take control.

15

VALUE WITHIN DESPAIR

"I would have lost heart, unless I had believed that I would see the goodness of the Lord in the land of the living. Wait on the Lord; be of good courage, and He shall strengthen your heart; wait, I say, on the Lord" **(Psalm 27:13, 14).**

As Joy put her life back together, she noticed a pattern. Every time she thought her spirit couldn't take another ounce of pain, she received an unexpected blessing. It was something as simple as a card from a friend whom she hadn't heard from in a while, or something substantial, such as a promotion at work. Some days it was an unexpected hug from Donovan when he knew she was drained. Another time, a car heading toward her when she stopped at the light swerved out of the way to avoid an accident. On another day, she lost a favorite earring and a coworker discovered it on the elevator and returned it. Joy quickly learned that even as her world had seemingly crumbled, God continued to send messages saying, "I have not abandoned or forgotten about you. My plans are for good and not evil; to give you hope and a future." God reassured her He was putting a plan in place for her to reach solid ground in the very near future. She recalled her mother saying to her when she first married, "If you pray, why worry? If you worry, why pray?"

The sadness, loneliness, and anger you feel after a relationship falls apart should prompt you at this stage to reexamine your life and the decisions that brought you to this phase. What made you stay in an abusive relationship? Was it insecurity, low self-esteem, fear, pride, intimidation, material possessions, sex, or nowhere to go and no one to turn to? Unless you realize what brought you to the relationship and held you captive, you will return to another one. If you continue to make the same mistakes, you'll continue to receive the same results. Use this time to evaluate your past, present, and future. Do you have daddy issues because your father wasn't in your life? Are you possessive? Are you controlling? Do you not feel worthy enough for a healthy relationship? Are you a know-it-all? Do you always *need* a man?

You were miserable in your relationship; your spirit was dying and you knew you had to rescue yourself or be rescued before it was too late. Upon leaving, you knew it wasn't going to be easy. So now you're here and you were right. It's still not easy. Know that the problems can be solved and the questions demand an answer.

When and how does it get easier? The answer is when you are ready to accept your portion of responsibility as well as the blessings in the midst of the despair; when you can look yourself in the mirror and say, "I did the best I could today Lord and You did the rest;" when you can say, "Lord, my kids just about drove me over the edge today, but I thank You they are asleep now;" or "Lord, my boss really got on my nerves today, but I thank You for providing employment and keeping Your hand over my mouth!"

Here's the message: in every sad situation, search for the goodness. Look through the pain for the blessings you might take for granted or miss at first glance. It makes the day go faster and certainly makes life more interesting. It's comparable to looking through a telescope at every cloud to find the silver lining. It's the spiritual game you play with God to see what He is hiding *for* you, not from you. And when you find it, all you can do is smile and thank Him for the many big and small surprises He has created.

Our God is extremely ingenious during times when both large and small dilemmas are expected. For instance, the Sunday after Joy moved into her new apartment, she decided the best place to start her new life was at church, especially since she hadn't been in months. She awoke early to have prayer and a light breakfast so she could arrive on time. Suddenly, she realized all of her clothes were folded in boxes. She had yet to purchase an ironing board, and had no idea where the iron was packed. She felt frustration emerging and thought that maybe this wasn't the Sunday to attend service. She knew clothes really didn't matter to God, but she wanted to look nice in public. As she reached into the first box, she pulled out a two-piece suit that looked like she had just picked it up from the cleaners— no wrinkles! She was shocked. How could a wool-blend suit, that had been folded and packed away for days, be wrinkle-free? The angels ironed my clothes, thought Joy with a smile. She laughed because she knew it could only be God's gesture, informing her that He was pleased that she intended to worship Him that morning at church. The rest of the day was exceptional; she was in good spirits and unpacked the remaining garments with amusement.

Joy recalls another miracle. Her nephew was getting married and it was her first big social event since the separation. She was nervous about her reaction to the wedding and prayed Donovan wouldn't get restless. Weddings can be joyous occasions for those who are getting married, but can generate painful memories for those whose marriage has exploded. Joy fell in the latter category. As she sat in the audience listening to the vows, her mind wandered to her own marriage, and how every promise was broken within the first five years. Lies, infidelity, physical and mental abuse were all there, but she stayed for twenty years. Where had God been in her marriage? Now she was on her own, beginning an excursion through the unhappy campground of domestic court. Joy was not a happy camper.

Naturally, she was relieved when the ceremony was over, largely because she was tired of smiling and pretending to be interested. As she tried to be sweet and courteous, she ignored the chatter of other guests who were probably speculating about her failed marriage. She left shortly after the reception began, pleased with the stellar performance she delivered as a happy, single mom.

The weather remained dry through the wedding, which was held in a beautiful park about twenty miles from home. As Joy drove home, rain suddenly pelted the windshield. It was late afternoon, and the downpour increased in intensity as she carefully navigated her way down the highway. With visibility decreasing, she wondered if she should pull over at the nearest exit.

All of a sudden Donovan yelled, "Mom, a double rainbow!"

Joy turned to the left and saw not one, but two magnificent rainbows hanging parallel in the sky. The sight was so luminous, she began to cry. Joy knew the vision was a gift from God to comfort her as she drove home. The colors were heavenly and gave her chills as she proceeded to her exit. It was a miracle only God could create and deliver at exactly the right time: a perfect ending to a less than perfect day...another kiss from God.

Month Three

16

FILL THE HOLE

"Now may the God of hope fill you with all joy and peace in believing, that you may abound in hope by the power of the Holy Spirit" (Romans 15:13).

Eva appreciated beautiful gardens but wasn't exactly experienced in how to go about landscaping a yard. She had a small lawn in front of her new duplex and the landlord was more than happy for her to spruce it up. Wanting to increase her knowledge, she carefully selected several gardening books at the library. She brimmed with excitement when purchasing several flats of marigolds, red impatiens, fertilizer, mulch, and a small shovel to dig the flower beds.

The twins couldn't wait to get up on Saturday morning and plant the flowers, for no other reason than it was an opportunity to get dirty without being scolded. By early afternoon, the trio, along with Sam, finished the planting, enjoying every minute of the hot sun as well as the occasional earthworm. They sipped lemonade on the small porch and basked in the neighbors' praise of their hard work. Within weeks, a few decided to add some color to their porches and yards. Eva and the girls had started a trend.

When you leave your spouse or significant other, there is a void, even if you have tumbled out of love. You notice a hole each time you find yourself in a place or activity that was a part of your married life or relationship. It feels strange and you don't quite know how to cope with it. It's a dull ache that makes you feel like you are in the wrong place at the wrong time. Companionship, whether good or bad, is missing. The cavity in your heart is greater than loneliness and needs a plug. What should you do?

Fill the hole. Fill your life with activities you considered doing when you didn't have the time, freedom, or luxury. Think about it. Can you learn to play the piano, read, write poetry or a book, attend plays, travel, join a women's club, start a home-based business, or return to school? Fill the hole in your life with activities that will make you a more interesting, global person. It's time for a tune-up of your mind, body, and spirit and every moment is precious. If you want to accomplish a goal or have a bucket list, put a plan in place.

When you emerge from this detox, you should be healthier, stronger, and a more intuitive person. You should know more about yourself because you have witnessed your weaknesses disappear into your strengths. You won't be enticed to attend a pity party because you have nothing to be pitiful about. Be proud of who you are. You have an opportunity to create the person you want to be and there is no better time than the present. You are a rare flower about to bloom.

17

SHARE YOUR LOVE

"I have shown you in every way, by laboring like this, that you must support the weak. And remember the words of the Lord Jesus, that He said, 'It is more blessed to give than to receive'" (Acts 20:35).

Kids are great but they grow up and have their own interests. More importantly, you need a life, especially if you don't have children. Some of the best advice we can give is to get a pet. Studies show that pets make great companions for those who are alone or disabled. When you are going through a divorce or separation, you may feel alone and disabled, but you aren't. A pet can deliver unconditional love when there is no one else. A dog or a cat can provide focus when you feel weak and ready for a pity party. Women are nurturing creatures and often need the emotional feedback from someone or something that expresses love for them. Pets can do this, and also give joy when you are feeling down and out.

If you are not a pet person, have allergies, or travel frequently, perhaps a new relationship with a young girl or elderly woman can offer new meaning to your life. There are thousands of young girls who need a "big sister" when their own mom is not available to help them mature or navigate the world. Big Brothers Big Sisters is an excellent agency to contact to start this process, or consider becoming a foster parent. Likewise, your church may have an active youth ministry in which you can become involved or support. The relationship will require at least a few visits per month, but often evolves into a close, lasting connection. By helping a young child grow, you can build her self-esteem and help her avoid negative relationships. As she depends on you, you realize how important it is to live up to your new image. You are a role model.

Elderly women need daughters when they are alone. Visit a nursing home and inquire who needs a make-believe daughter. There are many women who have outlived their families and have no visitors in their twilight years. Consider the Bible story of Ruth and Naomi. Living in the land of Moab, Naomi not only lost her husband, but her two sons who were married to Ruth and Orpah. Naomi urged her daughters-in-law to stay in Moab and remarry while she returned to her native Bethlehem. Ruth adamantly refused to leave her mother-in-law and accompanied Naomi on the long and treacherous journey back to Bethlehem. God rewarded Ruth's faithfulness to Naomi by blessing her with a wealthy husband, Boaz, who owned the fields where she happened to glean. Ruth's destiny was wrapped up in her care for and loyalty to Naomi and resulted in her place in Christ's lineage.

You may also miss your mother at this time if she is deceased or unable to give you motherly love. Generational love is God's way of preparing the children for tomorrow and the elderly for the afterlife. You have an important opportunity with either age group to put your life into perspective. What can you do to pay it forward, to be a blessing? Bless someone else and you will be blessed.

Your sister-friends can play an important part in sharing much needed love and companionship. They can serve as prayer partners, sounding boards, and companions when you exercise, travel, attend concerts, or simply hang out for dinner. Contemplate taking a mission trip together with your church or youth group. And when was the last time you did something fun together? When was that last pajama party?

18

A FOOD AFFAIR

"Who satisfies your mouth with good things, so that your youth is renewed like the eagle's" (Psalm 103:5).

Every night upon returning home from work, Eva had an affair—with the refrigerator. Initially after leaving Ellis, she lost several pounds. In an effort to put the weight back on, she made eating a priority. Food became her secret lover. She went to bed with food, she awoke to food, and kept something on her desk at work to snack on. Eva ate. Eva ate when she was bored, when she was nervous, and even when she wasn't the least bit hungry. She planned outings with associates and friends around restaurants and food events. Eva became a foodie. She weighed only ten pounds less than when she was pregnant with the twins, who as a result of Eva's poor diet, were also becoming unhealthy.

The day the invitation arrived in the mail for her twentieth high school class reunion snapped Eva out of the affair. At first, she was excited. Seeing old friends would be fun. She dug out the high school year book from the back of the closet and poured through the pages. As she came across photos of Greg, her high school sweetheart, the memories flooded back. Good memories. They were such a cute couple. She heard his wife died recently of a brain aneurism and she wondered if Greg would even attend the reunion. The thought of possibly seeing him again after all those years was exhilarating and yet scary. Eva wondered why they grew apart.

As she flipped through her closet, Eva couldn't find anything appropriate that fit. Everything was too snug to wear to a reunion. As she flung aside dress after dress, she knew it was either the scales or the mirror that would ultimately betray her. Was it the coffee cake in the morning, the cheeseburger with a side of fries, dinner *and* dessert, or the dish of ice cream to accompany a late night movie? She certainly didn't want to look like a circus tent in front of her old friends. Eva wanted to wear something with some panache. "Arrghhhh….the reunion is three months away," bemoaned Eva as she fell on the bed.

Your appearance is the first thing people see. Like it or not, we all have the tendency to make judgments about each other based on appearance. The images seen in the media aren't always kind to women. We come in different body types, height and weight. Nevertheless, you can be physically fit and attractive regardless of your frame.

As you age, you should pay more attention to your appearance. It is natural to gain weight due to menopause and changes in metabolism. Don't get in a rut mentally or physically. You don't have to look bad just because time is moving on. With time and a mental and physical plan, women can look good at any age.

Stay physically active so you can maintain your health and keep your body at its peak. The byproduct is that you will look and feel better about yourself. Get off the couch, leave the laptop behind, and get some fresh air. You can purchase three-, five- and eight-pound free weights for very little money, and a high-quality pair of gym shoes is always a good investment. The library holds exercise DVDs and Wii has games that offer great workout programs.

This is also a good time to take up a sport where you have previously been a spectator. Study it and do it. Get an accountability partner if you think you might quit, or join a support group.

Expand your horizons. Exercise does not have to be work and it can be fun. Gyms and church aerobic classes are great venues for connecting with people you might not otherwise meet. Exercise is a wholesome activity that can lead to better health, improved self-esteem, and new relationships. And, exercise will help you sleep better, especially if you are tired. Women who exercise as a lifestyle have improved health outcomes including lower blood pressure and cholesterol. Exercise also relieves stress and tension.

This is a good time to pick up good habits, not bad habits. What good habits have you ignored? Don't replace the holes in your life from a broken relationship with food, alcohol, or drugs. Since your body is a temple for God to dwell in, feed yourself with nutritious foods that promote a healthy lifestyle. Remember, feed your mind with His Word and love and blessings will surround you.

19

CREDIT WHERE CREDIT IS DUE

"And the Lord will make you the head and not the tail;
you shall be above only, and not be beneath, if you
heed the commandments of the Lord your God, which I
command you today, and are careful to observe them"
(Deuteronomy 28:13).

*J*oy was incredibly excited about finally getting dependable transportation. She had prayed her way to work for the last year, hoping the ten-year-old Chevy Blazer would make it one more mile. Winter was coming, and she knew there was transmission trouble on the way. Joy had taken one hundred dollars each month from her paycheck for a down payment. Today, with one thousand dollars in the bank, she was on her way to the Toyota dealer. She knew she couldn't afford a new car, but a late model Camry would be perfect for her and Donovan, maybe even with a sunroof.

After perusing the lot, Joy found the perfect car: two years old, low mileage with some warranty left, blue, and a sunroof. The price was a bit higher than she could afford, but perhaps the dealership would compromise. She told the salesman that she really liked the car but could only afford a payment of about two hundred and fifty dollars per month. He invited her into the showroom to talk to the finance manager about loan alternatives.

The finance manager completed a loan application online, and ran a credit report. Sitting comfortably in his office, Joy wasn't worried about her score; she always paid her bills on time. She expected to get a good rate, even if the payment was higher than she wanted. Unfortunately, the finance manager handed her the credit report, stating that the delinquencies on her accounts would not permit anything but high-risk pricing.

Staring at the credit report in disbelief, Joy wondered when and where did all the entries originate? She never knew about a gold American Express card or a Nordstrom account. Why were the accounts maxed out and past due? And why was the mortgage payment late? Jonathan had always handled the mortgage account when they were together and she faithfully deposited her paycheck into their account. She had just discovered another breach of her marriage vows: honesty. She couldn't believe Jonathan was so utterly dishonest and selfish. Now her credit was ruined and impacting the rate on a used car loan.

In hindsight, Joy wished she had opened every envelope that came into their home, whether it was personal or business. Then, she would have known how Jonathan used her name to secure additional credit. Her attorney told her that all assets or liabilities originating during the marriage were shared unless the application did not include information (such as social security number or employment data) on one of the partners.

Joy explained the situation to the finance manager and assured him that the delinquent accounts were not hers, but Jonathan's. Unfortunately, according to the finance manager, it didn't matter. It was on Joy's credit report, too, and Jonathan must have applied for joint credit. She thanked the finance manager and slowly walked away with the pain of the separation piercing her once again. She had promised herself months ago that she would not shed another tear for the past, but today she broke that commitment. Donovan was so excited about the possibility of a new car and now she had to tell him that this was not the best time. Jonathan had secretly supported his lavish lifestyle and rendezvous with credit cards and the mortgage money, leaving her to struggle to free herself from his frivolous and selfish choices. The whole situation wasn't fair or ethical, but she was determined to reach her goal.

Joy made an appointment with a credit counseling agency for help. Her divorce decree had not addressed this type of conflict, even though she thought her attorney had ordered a credit report on Jonathan during the trial. To address this situation, she would have to go back to court for further clarification, which would cost more money that she didn't have. Her misery seemed to never end, but someday her dream of a newer car would come true, even if she had to pay cash or a higher interest rate.

Her coworker suggested she try the credit union and explain her circumstances. They were willing to lend her eight thousand dollars with automatic payments from her paycheck for thirty-six months. To finalize the transaction, Joy offered to apply the one thousand dollars for a down payment, but that amount was insufficient to close the deal on the car she wanted. She settled for an older Camry that appeared to be in good shape, but with no sun roof. Thank God for the credit union! To stay on top of all her new obligations, Joy decided to put all bill payments in her calendar on her phone, and not spend a dime of her pay until all bills were current.

When a marriage ends, the joint credit history unfortunately may live on after the divorce is final. Divorce decrees should define which party is responsible for each debt and what should be done to the mortgage or rental property. Women should be involved in every aspect of the marital finances or any joint debt with a significant other. As a general rule, credit arrangements should remain separate until marriage or with an agreement of how to dispose of the debt if the partnership dissolves. Below are some rules to live by to avoid what Joy had to endure:

1. Check your credit report every year. Free credit reports can be obtained at annualcreditreport.com. Get one from Equifax, TransUnion, and Experian to compare entries.

2. Correct any discrepancies through written documentation, and keep copies of all correspondence. You have the right to dispute unfamiliar entries. Do this in writing. If the entry cannot be verified that it belongs to you, it should be removed from your report.

3. If there are major flaws, enter a statement on your credit report explaining the circumstance. This statement may not help with your credit score, but it will alert a lender that you are working to improve your credit rating.

4. If you leave a marriage, leave with copies of all financial arrangements: tax returns, credit cards, car loan information, mortgage/lease statements, personal financial statements, etc. You will need these for future reference.

5. Contact each creditor to discuss your relationship to see if anything can be done to separate you from your ex.

6. Discuss any undisclosed credit accumulated by your ex with your attorney to see if a contempt action is in order.

7. Start building new history with a secured card from a credit union or bank. Pay everything on time or before the due date. Pay more than the minimum and the overall interest paid will be less.

8. Avoid credit report clean-up scams. The best way to clean your score and improve your credit is to take control.

9. Communicate with all creditors in writing. Keep a record of all conversations and agreements with dates and names of the personnel with whom you are negotiating.

10. Negotiate lower interest rates if possible. If the rep on the phone can't or is unwilling to assist with lowering your rate, ask to speak to a manager.

    a. Change due dates to make it easier to make timely payments.

    b. Transfer credit card balances to cards with lower interest rates.

    c. Don't close paid off accounts, simply cut up the card—the longer the credit history, the higher your score can be.

11. Open a new bank account in your name only. Move all funds to which you are entitled from joint accounts to the new account. Compare rates and fees across banks. Credit unions are a good alternative if you have access to one.

12. Normally, you won't be able to purchase a new home until the marital residence is refinanced or sold. If the house or any other joint credit is in both names, be prepared for negative entries on your credit report, especially if your ex cannot or refuses to make payments on time. Pay your rent on time to build up a rental history to show you are responsible and independent from your ex.

13. Start a savings account for unforeseen expenses. Make it payroll deductible so it is automatically taken from your paycheck.

14. Write down the items that must be addressed each day and use your calendar to organize your life. You need systems so you don't forget a bill, a payment or important correspondence. Smart phones have excellent systems for recording and scheduling activities.

Yes, it's hard starting over, especially in the area of finances, but it can be done. Don't do it piece-meal; be strategic and thorough. Be detailed and timely. The separation of two lives must be comprehensive with emotional and legal boundaries. Progress is made each time you take one step toward your new and improved identity.

20

VICTORY

"For whatever is born of God overcomes the world. And this is the victory that has overcome the world—our faith" (I John 5:4).

*E*va was determined to finish the department's quarterly billing report before the deadline, and worked through lunch to be certain she had adequate time. To meet her goals, she practiced mental focus during the transition to singledom and became proficient at eliminating annoying distractions. This report would reflect her commitment to her job and attention to detail, in case coworkers suspected she had been negligent during the last several months.

Sensing someone's presence, Eva looked up from her computer to find her manager, Mark, staring down at her. "Eva, can I speak with you when you finish the report?"

"Of course," Eva said quickly. "I'll be done in about an hour."

Eva began to wonder what the meeting could possibly be about. Had she missed an important meeting or forgotten to submit a document? Did one of her nosy coworkers lie about her attendance? Maybe it was about her telephone usage. Admittedly, the twins called frequently when they needed permission for extracurricular activities or advice with homework. Eva sighed as she worked on the spreadsheet before her. Perhaps this would be her performance evaluation...no, that can't be; the last one was only six months ago. The hour passed quickly with random "what if" questions buzzing through her head, and Eva arrived at no solid conclusions for the impending meeting.

"Eva, I have watched your work over the last three months, and something has drastically changed," Mark observed as Eva nervously sat down across from him. "Your capacity for additional assignments has grown and others in our department look to you for advice. Recently, you have become one of my most trusted assistants and I have to know why. You seem to enjoy your position, but I believe you are ready for a higher level of responsibility. Tell me what happened that changed you so dramatically? I really need to get my other staff members to take a lesson from you."

Eva was speechless. She had no idea that Mark, or anyone else for that matter, noticed her new attitude. Secretly she had hoped word wasn't spreading about her separation from Ellis. Eva had lunched in the break room enough times to witness how stories were concocted, rumors spread, and outright lies were told.

Since leaving Ellis, she deliberately decided that excellence would be her standard in performance, dress, and demeanor. During the past few months, through prayer, reading the Word and taking advice from Natalie and her closest friends, God had blessed her with excellence. Eva stopped the whirlwind of thoughts about Ellis's mistreatment of her and the girls, realizing that his relationships with his stepmother and sister had always been strained. Maybe it was as simple as Ellis didn't like women. Ellis needed to work through his issues just as she was working through hers.

As a result of her new perspective on life, Eva solidly applied the principles of excellence to raising the twins, her environment, and her life's journey. In preparation for the anticipated high school reunion she became disciplined in her diet, and shed twelve pounds. Gradually her body was toning and she liked what she saw in the mirror. With her life on a completely different path, no longer did she see a battered and bruised woman, physically or spiritually. During that time, she painted the children's bedrooms, and cut her hair into a chic bob. The day of the high school reunion, Natalie convinced Eva to sit down at the department store cosmetic counter and chance a fresh make-over. After forty-five minutes, Eva looked stunning and couldn't believe how young she actually looked. With her renewed energy, Eva became secretary of the parent-teacher association for the upcoming school year. She felt and looked good, and it showed. God was standing up in her and she wondered why she had stayed in such an abusive relationship for so long.

"Mark, I was literally forced to make a decision a few months ago to make every day count. Every moment is precious and God has blessed me so abundantly that I wanted to demonstrate that I was worthy. I don't know if you are a Believer, but my explanation for any change is simple: God. Through the ups and downs of life, He always put my welfare first and I am simply grateful to work here, go home to my kids, and live a healthy, productive life," Eva replied.

Mark sat back and smiled. "Well, I knew something had changed and I needed to hear firsthand. I also want you to know that you are my choice for Employee of the Month. I can also see a promotion for you in the near future. Eva, thanks for your service to our firm."

At the close of the day, Eva quickly gathered her belongings to make sure she was on time for the parent-teacher conference at the children's school. There was enough warmth from the sun to welcome her as she zipped through the double-glass doors. To her surprise, there stood Ellis with a bouquet of daffodils, her favorite flower. Stopping dead in her tracks, Eva shielded her eyes from the sun's rays as she contemplated her next move. She decided to keep walking.

"Ellis, what do you want?" Eva asked picking up her stride. "I've got a meeting and you will not make me late!" Unbelievable. Just as I'm getting my life back, here he comes, thought Eva to herself. And he must have forgotten about the restraining order.

"Wow, Eva, you look beautiful," Ellis said nervously. "I know you haven't heard from me in a while and you have every reason to hate me, but I've wanted to tell you for the last several weeks that I am truly sorry for how I treated you and how I neglected Camille and Cara, then and now. The three of you are the best things that have happened to me and I couldn't see it while we were together. Despite what you think, I love you and now I know I always will." Ellis paused and took a breath.

"I can't ask you to forget what I've done over the years, but do you think you could ever forgive me?" Ellis clutched the flowers, forgetting to hand them to Eva. "Maybe we can start with small steps for the girls and see what happens," he said, with his voice trembling.

For the second time that afternoon, Eva was speechless. She had rarely seen or talked to Ellis during the last two months. He faithfully paid the court-mandated child support, but hadn't spent much time with the twins. He looked tired and nervous, and she really believed he had rehearsed his speech to make sure he wasn't snarky or put his foot in his mouth. Eva had dreamed of this day many times and her heart beat wildly. During the last few months, she had examined their marriage over and over— the strengths and weaknesses. Clearly, their marriage lacked mutual respect, consideration, and patience. Ellis's troubled upbringing left scars of isolation and neglect Eva was not prepared to handle. She was no longer naive and Eva aspired for a relationship that included unconditional love and a commitment. A line was drawn in the sand and Ellis was on the other side. Never again would Eva accept a love deficient or void of God's standards.

Despite the scenarios she had played out in her head, she knew this time God wanted her to trust Him and not Ellis. Throughout the last few months, Eva witnessed the outpouring of God's unconditional love through His provision and His peace. Her new identity in Christ gave cause for celebration and she had a godly pride about who she was and where she was going. This was not the time to regress.

Eva was in a hurry. "Ellis, what do you *really* want? You haven't seen or talked to the twins in weeks, so slow your row," snapped Eva, with her hand on her hip, head tilted to the side. "If anything, this should be the time for you to connect with your children, don't you think? And for once you're right. You seriously hurt me in ways that I will never forget. I've been working on forgiving you since we left that night, and I'm not there yet. It will come in time. But you... you have some serious issues that you must immediately address."

Eva paused and exhaled deeply. Unlike the past, today she was in control and needed to keep it that way. She deserved the best, and in this or any other relationship, she would demand it. If Ellis were to come back into their lives, it would be on God's terms, not his.

"Tell you what. Why don't you pick up the girls at Barbara's while I attend this meeting? I'll call her and let her know you're coming. My meeting shouldn't last more than an hour. Then maybe we can grab a bite to eat and you can explain to the girls what's been going on with you. We'll pray about what happens next."

Ellis smiled through his disappointment. He had no choice but to go along with Eva's program. Sitting in the house night after night presented him with time to face his dreams and his failures. Time to think about the people, especially the women, he hurt over the years. Time to think about the people he considered important and valuable and what he was going to do with the balance of his life. The house was quiet and empty, and the only sounds he heard were the voices running around in his head. Reflecting on his life, Ellis uncovered a pattern of fractured relationships with the women in his childhood, adolescence, and adulthood. Raised by a strict stepmother, Ellis competed with three other siblings for love and attention. His father worked two jobs and didn't have the capacity to offer emotional support. Ellis never learned the art of love, of selfless giving, or how to nurture a relationship. Hanging out in the clubs had practically worn him out and he came to the realization that most of the women hanging on his arm were there for the free drinks and nothing more. He was tired of the whole scene and desired to come home to soft music and his wife and children.

Ellis had lost women before, but not one of them was Eva. Eva had a gift for attracting kindness and love from family and friends. Truth be told, Ellis was slightly jealous of how easily Eva loved and the way the girls brightened when she entered a room. He had to own up to making a mess of his marriage and potentially damaging a relationship with his daughters, primarily because he was insecure and needed to be in control of everything and everyone around him. The steep and delicate climb back into Eva's life would not be easy, but it would be well worth the effort and certainly uncharted territory for Ellis.

Ninety days. You made it! Your victory is a result of faith in God, faith in yourself, and the ability to forgive your abuser. You may never forget what happened, but you can remove the hatred through forgiveness. God forgave you, didn't he? He carried you from confusion to contentment, from pain to prosperity, from pity to praise, and from drama and doubt to determination. Your life is becoming enriched and you should be walking in a season of receiving, maintaining, and releasing God's blessings.

Life isn't perfect and God never promised perfection. His Word says that His strength is made perfect in our weakness. Every day counts, whether your goals come in bits and pieces or milestones.

Keep your head up and look forward. Don't be like Lot's wife and look back. Your destiny is ahead, not behind, and you are an example of the power that comes when you invest in God and not man. The dawn of each morning is purposed to shower you with joy and the anticipation of another dimension of God's unfailing love. With Christ all things are possible.

You are a priceless work of art, a precious masterpiece. Don't be surprised when friends and family comment that something is different about you. There is.

"The Spirit of the Lord God is upon me, because the Lord has anointed me to preach good tidings to the poor; He has sent me to heal the brokenhearted, to proclaim liberty to the captives, and the opening of the prison to those who are bound; to proclaim the acceptable year of the Lord, and the day of vengeance of our God; to comfort all who mourn, to console those who mourn in Zion, to give them beauty for ashes, the oil of joy for mourning, the garment of praise for the spirit of heaviness; that they may be called trees of righteousness, the planting of the Lord, that He may be glorified" *(Isaiah 61: 1-3).*

21

NATIONAL RESOURCES

Credit/debt/bankruptcy Counseling: Apprisen Financial Services, www.apprisen.com

Consumer fraud: Federal Trade Commission Consumer Protection Agency

http://www.ftc.gov/bcp/index.shtml

Federally insured health and dental clinics – check for those in your local area

Housing programs: U.S. Department of Housing and Urban Development (HUD)

http://portal.hud.gov/

Food assistance: Government Benefits Online.org

http://www.govbenefitsonline.org/

The Legal Aid Society: www.legal-aid.org

Women's empowerment: YWCA (physical fitness, classes, daycare) www.ywca.org

Community colleges offer an array of courses and services at low cost.

Check local beauty colleges/schools for low cost beauty services.

Contact your local city attorney's office for protection orders, etc.

Domestic Violence Resources

This list is by no means comprehensive. It is a starting point. Websites, and the information they contain, come and go, so please keep your resources updated.

- An Abuse, Rape, and Domestic Violence Aid and Resources Collection: (AARDVARC): aardvarc.org

- Bottomless Closet: www.bottomlessclosetnyc.org. This site connects women and work in Chicago and New York.

- Breaking the Cycle: www.breakingthecycle.org. The mission is to empower youth to end the cycle of domestic violence.

- Cut it Out: www.cutitout.org. This is a program of Salons Against Domestic Violence Abuse Fund. It has trained more than 40,000 salon workers in all 50 states to recognize signs of domestic abuse. Domestic Abuse Helpline for Men and Women: www.dahmw.org, 1-888-743-5754.

- Dress for Success: www.dressforsuccess.org. Promotes economic independence of disadvantaged women by providing professional attire, a network of support and career development tools. The agency has international and national affiliates.

- FACE to FACE: A joint program of The National Coalition Against Domestic Violence Project and the Academy of Facial and Plastic Reconstructive Surgery. Provides free reconstructive surgery for victims of domestic violence, male and female. Call 1-800-842-4546.

- Give Back a Smile Program: This program is dedicated to providing cosmetic dental care at no cost to all survivors of domestic violence. www.aacd.com, or call 1-800-773-4227.

- Jewish Women International: www.jwi.org

- MenWeb: www.batteredmen.com. This site offers resources for men and an opportunity to tell their story.

- National Coalition Against Domestic Violence: www.ncadv.org
- National Network to End Domestic Violence: www.nnedv.org
- Pandora's Project:
  Offers support and resources for survivors of rape and sexual abuse. www.pandys.org
- The National Domestic Violence Hotline: 1-800-799-7233
- The National Sexual Assault Hotline: 1-800-656-4673
- The National Teen Dating Abuse Hotline: 1-866-331-9474, 1-866-331-8453 TTY, or text "loveis" to 77054
- The U.S. Department of Justice Office on Violence Against Women Grant Programs: This federal agency funds 21 programs. Go to http://www.ovw. usdoj.gov/ovwgrantprograms.htm#18
- www.dosomething.org: Has a focus on healthy teen relationships
- www.loveisrespect.org: Focuses on teen and young adult dating and abuse
- www.womenslaw.org: This site has numerous resources

ABOUT THE AUTHORS

Iris Ann Cooper

Iris Ann Cooper hails from Evansville, Indiana. From her career in business, she has developed an expertise in the management of a variety of projects for businesses, nonprofits, and government. Her principles are education, economic empowerment, entrepreneurship, and equality for all people. She enjoys writing, art, music, travel, and fitness to achieve work-life balance.

She is the owner of JustAskIris!, an entrepreneurial consulting firm. Iris is one of the founders of Glory Foods, Inc., a national food marketing company, and has also operated a mortgage business and retail gift shop. Her column "The Bottom Line" appears in GrapevineColumbus.com with commentary on small business issues. Her column and radio show *Just Ask Iris* provided business information to the Columbus market for many years. She continues to speak nationally on business and economic development matters.

Iris is the former chair of the Economic Empowerment Committee for the National Coalition of 100 Black Women. She was featured in the October 2008 issue of *Entrepreneur Magazine* and chosen as a 2008 Woman of Economic and Leadership Development. Additionally, she was honored in 2006 as a YWCA Woman of Achievement. She is a member of Alpha Kappa Alpha Sorority, Inc., the Academy of Management, and the Central Ohio Chapter of the Coalition of 100 Black Women.

Iris obtained a Bachelor of Arts degree in journalism and a Master of Business Administration degree in marketing from Indiana University. She is "ABD" in the Doctor of Business Administration program at Walden University, majoring in entrepreneurship. She teaches business courses at Franklin University and Columbus State Community College. Her family includes her children Mica and Malik, and her precious grandson Malachi.

Visit her at www.justaskiris.com
LinkedIn: http://www.linkedin.com/profile/view?id=41031429

Melanie Houston

Melanie Houston is a publisher, an author and the founder and Chief Executive Officer of Alabaster Box Media Group, a division of Vision Resources, Inc. Alabaster Box Media Group is a multimedia company dedicated to publishing, producing, and promoting literary and artistic works that advance the Gospel of Jesus Christ. She also serves as the Chief Operating Officer of Daniel Houston & Associates.

Melanie's professional background includes human resource and management experience that exceeds thirty years in corporate America and with her own management consulting firm. Clients include national and international profit and nonprofit organizations in the areas of community service, publishing, energy, telecommunications, microelectronics and chambers of commerce. She has served as an executive editor for an award-winning national publishing house, an international magazine, and several independent publishers. Charting her journey as a publisher, *Rivers of Grace: Poems of Redemption and Restoration* was Alabaster Box Media Group's first release.

A native of Columbus, Ohio, Melanie graduated from Capital University with a Bachelor of Arts degree in art therapy. She received a Master of Arts degree from The Ohio State University, with a major in labor and human resource management.

Melanie is a member of the Women's Service Board of the King Arts Complex and a Kids Coach for Future Possibilities, Inc. In her spare time she enjoys creating works of art, jewelry design, travel, and reading a good book.

She celebrates the covenant of marriage with the extraordinary Daniel Houston. Together they share a daughter, Alexis, son-in-law, Marlon, and grandchildren Aries and Mason.

Visit her at www.alabasterboxmedia.com

LinkedIn:http://www.linkedin.com/profile/view?id=27103690&trk=nav_responsive_tab_profile

"And when Jesus was in Bethany at the house of Simon the leper, a woman came to him having an alabaster flask of very costly fragrant oil, and she poured it on His head as He sat at the table. But when His disciples saw it, they were indignant saying, "Why this waste? For this fragrant oil might have been sold for much and given to the poor."

But when Jesus was aware of it, He said to them, "Why do you trouble the woman? For she has done a good work for Me. For you have the poor with you always, but Me you do not have always. For in pouring the fragrant oil on My body, she did it for My burial. Assuredly, I say to you, wherever this gospel is preached in the whole world, what this woman has done will also be told as a memorial to her."

Matthew 26:6-13

This book is also available as an e-book.
Visit http://www.smashwords.com/

Speaking Engagements

Iris Cooper and Melanie Houston are available for speaking engagements on the topic of domestic violence, intimate partner abuse and implementing a 90-day plan to recover from domestic abuse.

For speaking engagements contact:

Iris Cooper: iris@justaskiris.com or call 614.750.1870

Melanie Houston: melanie@alabasterboxmedia.com
or call 614.432.0702

Workshops for Churches, Faith-based and Other Organizations

Workshops are presented in three-hour and six-hour formats. They are for women who are victims, who know someone who is a victim, have witnessed the broken remains of a survivor, or who suspect someone has fallen victim to domestic violence.
Topic: Strategies for overcoming the effects of domestic violence using biblical principles and safe practices. The workshop will include discussion of a 90-day plan for survival and recovery.

Workshop for Helping Professionals on Culture and Domestic Violence

Presented by Dan Houston, Daniel Houston & Associates

The workshop will define violence and risk factors within a cultural framework. It will also review the most common psychological problems associated with women of color including substance abuse, depression, suicide attempts and physical health problems. Additionally, the workshop explores prevention, intervention and advocacy options from research and community-based perspectives.